James Martin's
AMERICAN ADVENTURE

Dedicated to the late great Antonio Carluccio.
The world lost a good man and I lost a good friend.
Rest in peace.

James Martin's AMERICAN ADVENTURE

80 CLASSIC AMERICAN RECIPES

Photography by Peter Cassidy

quadrille

Publishing director: Sarah Lavelle
Commissioning editor: Céline Hughes
Project editor: Amy Christian
Creative director: Helen Lewis
Art direction and design: Smith & Gilmour
Photography: Peter Cassidy
Food preparation and styling: James Martin, Sam Head and Chris Start
Props stylist: Rebecca Newport
Home economists: Sam Head and Emma Marsden
Production: Tom Moore and Vincent Smith

First published in 2018 by Quadrille, an imprint of Hardie Grant Publishing
Quadrille, 52–54 Southwark Street, London, SE1 1UN

quadrille.com

10 9 8 7 6 5 4 3 2 1

Text © 2018 James Martin

Photography © 2018 Peter Cassidy

Design and layout © 2018 Quadrille Publishing

Cataloguing in Publication Data: a catalogue record for this book
is available from the British Library.

ISBN: 978 178713 153 8

Printed in Germany

Recipe note:
Ingredients are listed in UK
metric, followed by US cups/
imperial measurements.
Please use just one system
of measurement when
following the recipes.

CONTENTS

INTRODUCTION

So why America? What can Americans teach us when it comes to food? Sure, everyone thinks of Italy and France – and now Japan – as culinary centres, but America, really?

You would be wrong, very wrong, to think that America comes way down the pecking order when it comes to the quality of their food. Forget pretzels and doughnuts, this place has so much more to offer.

I set off on my journey to show you how good this place is and it didn't disappoint. With a country so vast, it was difficult to know where to start, let alone which route to take. As the team and I sat in the UK looking at a large map of the country, I had several places in mind – some that I had been to before, and some that I had never visited.

With a few pins in the East coast and a few in the West, we set off on the trip, topping and tailing with visits to chefs and places I'd been before. On the West coast, top of the list was The French Laundry, run by Thomas Keller, the only US chef to hold two 3-star restaurants and in whose restaurant I ate one of the greatest meals I have ever had. I also called Wolfgang Puck ('Mr Los Angeles'), probably the most famous chef in the US, asking if he would be a part of the trip. Twenty-three weeks later we were in Beverly Hills being cooked for by him and his team.

Six weeks later, we hit the East coast to meet two more masters of their craft. Daniel Boulud and Éric Ripert are giants of the New York food scene. Both have Michelin stars coming out of their ears and both have restaurants that are regularly in the 'Top 10' lists around the world.

I knew these places would be great, and they didn't let us down, but along the road we also found many new places that surprised me. Take the Single Thread in Sonoma, run by husband-and-wife team Kyle and Katina Connaughton, fast becoming the most talked-about eatery in California, if not the whole of the US. Congrats go out to them as they have just been awarded two Michelin stars, only a few months after opening. They have one of the most beautiful dining rooms I have ever been in – it's a must if you go to the US.

But it was 'Middle America' that surprised me the most in so many ways. The people were amazing and so friendly, the produce so diverse and the countryside stunning. It was not all cowboys and pick-up trucks (although in Dallas cowboy boots are a must!). It's the food and drink I will remember. For some of our crew, take Toppy the cameraman, it's the drink he'll remember more than anything – New Orleans took its toll on him. And Matt, the soundman, now knows never to eat fresh Szechuan peppercorns in a Santa Cruz market.

It was the places that we went – some of them off piste from the route we had marked on our map back home – that made the trip so special. The markets and food shops were amazing. The produce grown along the roadside didn't disappoint. The smells along the coast of sea air and strawberry fields coupled with the artichoke farms of Santa Cruz. Some of the best wine in the world in the vineyards of Napa and Sonoma. Plus who would have thought that Tabasco came from an island of salt? Angelo's had the best BBQ in the US and a trip to the massive Billy Bob's is a must, to watch a bit of armadillo racing after a quick line dance.

Forget politics – it's the people that make America great. They couldn't have been nicer, couldn't have been more friendly and the produce couldn't have been better to cook with. For that, America, I want to thank you. Thank you for one of the best trips of my life and for allowing me (I hope) to help to change people's perception of American food. I came back to the UK thinking sure, America has some rubbish places and, my God, some odd things to eat, but it does also have some of the best food in the world. I really think so.

And if you make the trip following the same rule that I did – never to eat anything that's bigger than your head – you will come back only a few pounds heavier than when you left and with a view of their food which will change you forever. The crew's perception of American food changed completely in just the six weeks we were there. My director turned to me while taking his bag off the carousel at Heathrow and said 'Thanks Jay, I loved it. Six weeks ago I thought the best food in America was at Hooters, so thanks.'

There you go... compliments indeed.

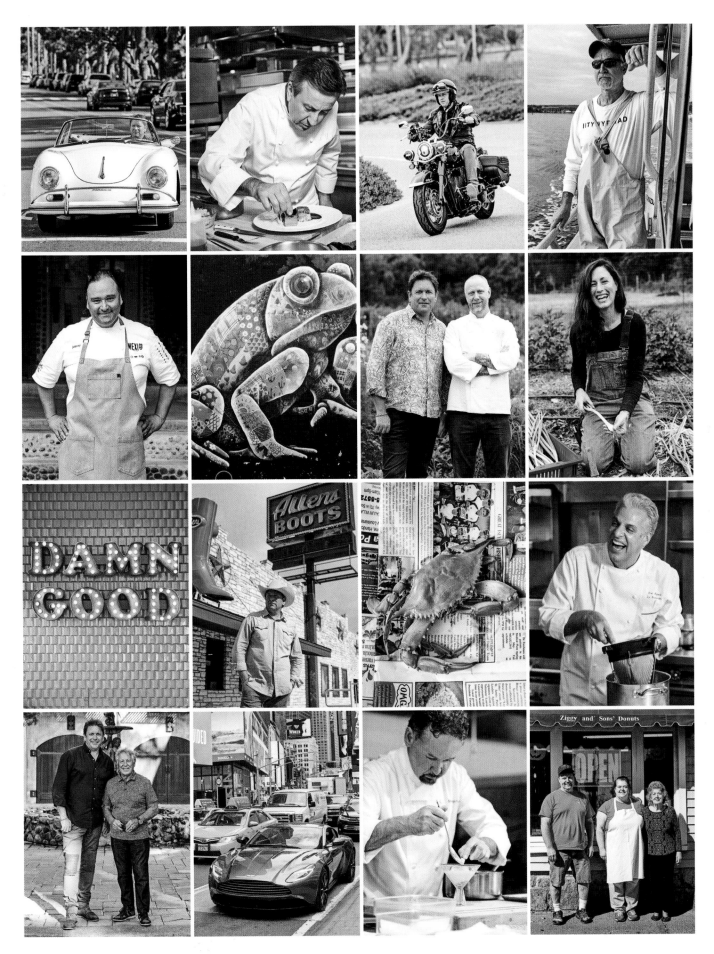

BREAKFAST
& BRUNCH

Brunch doesn't get much more American than this – muffins topped with Canadian bacon, poached egg and hollandaise. This classic dish is said to have originated at Delmonico's in lower Manhattan, where it was made for a Mr Benedict, a retired Wall Street stockbroker.

EGGS BENEDICT

=== SERVES 4 ===

4 large eggs
1 teaspoon olive oil
2 English muffins, halved
200g (7 oz) spinach, washed
8 slices cooked Canadian
    bacon or ham

For the hollandaise sauce
1 large egg yolk
1 teaspoon white wine vinegar
300g (1⅓ cups) clarified butter
sea salt and freshly ground
    black pepper

To serve
1 teaspoon freshly chopped chives

Fill a bowl with water and a handful of ice cubes. Next, pour enough water into a large saucepan so it's about a third of the way up the side and bring to the boil. Use a whisk to create a fast whirl and carefully drop one egg into the water. Cook for 2–3 minutes. Lift out with a slotted spoon then drop the egg into the iced water to cool quickly. Now drain on a plate lined with kitchen paper. Repeat with the remaining eggs.

To make the hollandaise sauce, whisk the egg yolk and vinegar together in a large heatproof bowl. Place over the same pan of boiling water, making sure that the base doesn't touch the water. Add the butter, a drizzle at a time, whisking continuously until the mixture thickens. Season with salt and black pepper. Take the bowl off the pan and keep warm. Keep the pan of water to one side – you'll need it to dip the eggs in to reheat them in a while.

Heat a large frying pan until hot, drizzle in the olive oil and place the muffins cut-side down to toast them. Place to one side.

Add the spinach to the same pan and cook until wilted. Lower each poached egg into the hot water for 30 seconds to warm through.

To serve, pop a muffin half each on four plates, top with the spinach, then with the bacon or ham. Place the poached egg on top, spoon over the sauce and sprinkle with the chives.

Also from Delmonico's in Manhattan comes this dish, made with cream, sherry, cognac, eggs and cayenne pepper. There are lots of varieties of this classic – some with cream and some without – but the use of egg yolks to thicken the sauce is a must. Don't overcook it otherwise it will become lobster scrambled egg Newburg.

LOBSTER NEWBURG

≡ SERVES 2 ≡

2 teaspoons olive oil
1 English muffin, halved
200g (7 oz) baby leaf
　spinach, washed
1 shallot, diced
400g (14 oz) cooked lobster,
　cut into 5cm (2 in) chunks
2 tablespoons sherry
2 tablespoons brandy
pinch of cayenne pepper
sea salt and freshly ground
　black pepper
4 tablespoons hot
　chicken stock
100ml (½ cup) double
　(heavy) cream
2 medium egg yolks
1 teaspoon freshly chopped
　chives, plus extra to
　garnish (optional)

In a large non-stick frying pan, heat half the oil and toast the muffin halves on both sides. Set aside on a plate.

In the same pan, wilt the spinach for 30 seconds, then transfer to a bowl.

In the same pan, add the remaining oil and fry the shallot for 1 minute. Stir in the lobster then add the sherry, brandy and cayenne and season well. Flambé the sherry and brandy to burn off the alcohol.

Stir in the hot stock and half the cream and simmer to reduce by half.

Pour the remaining cream into a small bowl and whisk in the egg yolks. Whisk together then pour into the pan with the lobster. Reduce the heat and cook very gently until thickened. Taste for seasoning and stir through the chives.

Place a muffin half each onto two plates. Divide the spinach evenly between the two muffins, then top with the lobster. Spoon any sauce over at the end and serve with a few chives on top.

A cross between a muffin and a croissant, cruffins are said to have originated in San Francisco. They can be filled or topped with a variety of flavourings, and are often served with whipped cream on top.

BLUEBERRY CRUFFINS

140g (2 cups minus 2 teaspoons) cold unsalted butter, chopped into sugar-cube-sized pieces, plus extra to grease

225g (1⅔ cups) strong white bread flour, plus extra for shaping

2 tablespoons golden caster (superfine) sugar

1 teaspoon lemon juice

1 teaspoon fresh yeast or ½ teaspoon dried yeast

125ml (½ cup) warm water

1 medium egg, beaten

100g (¾ cup) blueberries

icing (powdered) sugar, for dusting

Grease and line a 12-hole muffin tin or use a silicone muffin mould.

Sift the flour into the bowl of a freestanding mixer fitted with a dough hook. Add the sugar, a quarter of the butter and the lemon juice. Stir together.

Mix the yeast with half the water and set aside for a few minutes for the yeast to activate. Pour into the bowl, start the machine running at medium speed and pour in the rest of the water slowly, mixing for about 1 minute.

Once the dough has combined, tip onto a lightly floured surface and knead for a minute. Place the dough back into a clean bowl, cover with clingfilm (plastic wrap) and leave to rise until doubled in size, around 30–40 minutes.

Once the dough has risen, tip onto a floured surface. Cut the dough in half, then roll half of it through a pasta machine on the largest setting, using the slowest setting. Coat in flour and repeat.

Spread half the remaining butter over half the dough and fold over, flour, roll out to an oblong and put through the pasta machine again. Roll up into a cigar shape along the length of the dough to make one long cigar. Cut down the middle, around two-thirds of the way through, then flip it back on itself so the cut side is on the outside and the non-cut edges are on the middle. Cut into 6 shorter pieces along the length, then roll each piece up so it looks like a pinwheel. Push into a muffin hole then do the same until you've filled 6 holes. Repeat with the remaining dough and butter, filling all the muffin holes. Leave to prove for about 1 hour.

Preheat the oven to 160°C/325°F/gas mark 3.

Brush with the beaten egg and sprinkle with blueberries and bake in the oven for 20–25 minutes. Remove from the tin, cool on a wire rack then dust with icing (powdered) sugar and serve.

As anyone who has been to the States will know, ordering pancakes for breakfast can often feel like taking part in an eating challenge of some kind. Usually the pancakes are stacked up, six high per person, and are about the size of dustbin lids. Mine aren't quite so large, in line with my motto on the trip: never eat anything bigger than your head!

BLUEBERRY & BOURBON PANCAKES

MAKES 12 (SERVES 4)

For the compote
500g (4 cups) blueberries
50g (¼ cup) caster (superfine) sugar
2 tablespoons bourbon whiskey

For the pancakes
75g (⅓ cup) butter
200g (1½ cups) plain (all-purpose) flour
50g (¼ cup) caster (superfine) sugar
1 teaspoon baking powder
3 medium eggs, beaten
200ml (1 cup) buttermilk

To serve
200ml (1 cup) double (heavy) cream, lightly whipped
100ml (½ cup) maple syrup

Place three-quarters of the blueberries in a saucepan and add the caster (superfine) sugar and bourbon whiskey. Place over a medium heat, bring to a simmer and cook gently for 5 minutes.

Melt one-third of the butter in a small pan. Pour into a bowl, cool a little and add the flour, sugar and baking powder. Give everything a stir to mix roughly, then add the beaten eggs and buttermilk. Whisk the mixture until smooth, then stir in the remaining blueberries.

In a large frying pan, melt a quarter of the remaining butter over a low to medium heat. Once the butter has stopped foaming, spoon in three large spoonfuls of the mixture, spaced apart, and cook for 1 minute. Flip each one over and cook for a further minute. Transfer to a warmed plate and keep warm. Repeat this process until all the butter has been used up and the batter has been cooked.

To serve, divide the pancakes among the plates, spoon over the blueberry compote, dollop on the whipped cream and finally drizzle over the maple syrup.

This is a go-to meal in the States. Waffles are so easy to cook and make, and are great when coupled with this simple tomato soup. The whole dish can be made in less than ten minutes.

CHEESY BACON WAFFLES WITH TOMATO SOUP

=== SERVES 4 ===

For the waffles
100g (3½ oz) streaky bacon, diced
100g (½ cup minus 1 tablespoon) salted butter, melted, plus an extra knob
250g (2 cups) plain (all-purpose) flour
1 tablespoon caster (superfine) sugar
1 teaspoon baking powder
1 teaspoon salt
3 medium eggs
200ml (1 cup) milk
200g (2 cups) grated Cheddar cheese

For the tomato soup
3½ tablespoons olive oil, plus extra for drizzling
1 shallot, diced
1 garlic clove, chopped
2 x 400g (14 oz) tins chopped tomatoes
12 basil leaves, plus extra for serving
pinch of caster (superfine) sugar
sea salt and freshly ground black pepper

You will also need a waffle machine

Preheat the waffle machine until hot.

Heat a medium frying pan until hot and dry-fry the bacon pieces until golden. Add a knob of butter, allow to melt, then take off the heat and cool.

Put the flour into a large bowl, then add the sugar, baking powder, salt, eggs, milk, melted butter and cooked bacon. Whisk everything together to a dropping consistency.

Ladle into the waffle machine – be careful not to overfill. Close the lid and cook for a couple of minutes until golden and crispy. Continue to cook the waffles until you've used all the mixture up.

To make the tomato soup, heat the oil in a medium saucepan and sweat the shallot and garlic for 1–2 minutes. Add the tomatoes and 4 tablespoons of water, cover and bring to the boil and add the basil. Add a pinch of sugar and season, then drizzle with olive oil. Simmer for 4–5 minutes.

Preheat the grill (broiler). Put the waffles on a large baking tray, cover in cheese and grill until golden and bubbling. Cut the waffles into triangles.

Meanwhile, blitz the soup until smooth with a heatproof stick blender (or cool a little and put in a food processor). Warm through over a low heat.

To serve, ladle the soup into warm bowls, drizzle with olive oil, sprinkle over the basil and serve with the cheesy waffles.

This was inspired by a trip to Turner's Seafood restaurant in Salem, where I had the best clam pasta I have ever tasted, cooked on clam steamers in full view directly behind the bar. As you entered the restaurant you could buy a whole range of locally caught seafood, including the famous East Coast Maine lobster. This is a really simple dish of lobster on toast, with a lovely cheese-based sauce.

SEAFOOD ON TOAST

=== SERVES 2 ===

knob of salted butter
100g (3½ oz) spinach, washed
sea salt and freshly ground pepper
extra virgin olive oil, for drizzling
4 slices sourdough bread
2 medium egg yolks
375ml (2½ cups) full-fat
  crème fraîche
1 tablespoon Dijon mustard
25g (1 oz) Parmesan cheese,
  grated, plus extra to sprinkle
200g (7 oz) prawns (shrimp),
  cooked and shelled
600g (1 lb 5 oz) clams, cooked
  and meat picked out of shells
1 lobster, cooked and meat
  removed

Place a medium saucepan over a medium heat and add the butter. Once the butter has melted and is foaming, add the spinach to the pan and cook until wilted. Season, then spoon into a sieve resting over a bowl to drain.

Heat a large frying pan over a medium heat. Drizzle the olive oil over the bread and toast until golden, then flip over and toast the other side.

Beat the egg yolk, crème fraîche and mustard together in a small bowl, season, then fold in the grated Parmesan.

Preheat the grill (broiler). Layer the spinach, prawns (shrimp), clams and lobster on top of the toast then spoon over the crème fraîche mixture. Grate more Parmesan over the top and place under the grill for a minute until golden and bubbling, then serve.

STARTERS, SOUPS & STREET FOOD

This is a quick and easy dish to make. You simply need salt, sugar and an alcohol of your choice. I like gin but you could also use whiskey or bourbon. The idea for this dish came from Spirit Works, a small independent distillery, owned by a Brit, that we visited in Sonoma.

GIN-CURED SALMON
WITH PICKLED CAULIFLOWER

≡ SERVES 8-10 ≡

200g (1 cup) caster (superfine) sugar
200g (7 oz) table salt
4 tablespoons rice wine vinegar
100ml (½ cup) gin
200g (7 oz) cauliflower, cut into small florets
200g (7 oz) romanesco cauliflower, cut into small florets
1 side of salmon, approx. 1.5kg (3¼ lb)
12 fig leaves (optional)
175g (6 oz) piccalilli

To make the pickle, put 2 tablespoons sugar into a saucepan with 2 tablespoons salt, 4 tablespoons vinegar and 3 tablespoons gin.

Place over a medium heat and bring to a simmer to dissolve the sugar and salt, then take the pan off the heat. Add the cauliflower and romanesco and pour into a bowl.

To cure the salmon, check that all the bones have been removed – use tweezers to pull up vertically.

Mix the remaining salt and sugar together in a bowl. Cover a large board with three layers of clingfilm (plastic wrap). Cover the middle with fig leaves (if using), and pour over one-sixth of the salt and sugar mixture. Lay the salmon flesh-side down on top of the salt. Cover in more fig leaves and more salt and sugar mixture.

Douse with gin and wrap tightly in the clingfilm. Do the same again with the other side of salmon. Refrigerate for 24 hours.

The next day, rinse the salt and sugar mixture off the salmon under cold running water and pat the flesh dry with kitchen paper.

Blitz the piccalilli in a small food processor until smooth.

To remove the skin from the salmon, lay one of the sides on a board, flesh-side up. Insert a fish filleting knife at the tail end at a 30-degree angle and wiggle between the skin and the flesh. Holding the end of the tail firmly down on the board, slide the knife along the skin to slice it off the fillet. Next, remove the blood line; this is the thin line that runs along the centre of the salmon fillet – just carefully cut along each side of it and pull away.

Cut the salmon into 1cm (½ in) slices, and place three of the slices on each plate with the smooth piccalilli and the pickle.

Almonds and avocado are two of the most popular ingredients that come out of California. In fact it's official – they are the state nut and fruit. This recipe is for a simple guac with the chicken and the shrimp panéed in a mixture of almonds and breadcrumbs. The shrimp and chicken need to be cut into bite-sized pieces, so they cook quickly (and are easier to eat!).

POPCORN CHICKEN & SHRIMP
WITH AN ALMOND CRUMB & GUACAMOLE

SERVES 6–8

For the chicken and shrimp
1 litre (5 cups) vegetable oil,
  for deep-frying
150g (3½ cups) panko
  breadcrumbs
150g (2 cups) flaked (slivered)
  almonds, roughly chopped
170g (1¼ cups) plain
  (all-purpose) flour
3 medium eggs, beaten
400g (14 oz) large raw prawns
  (shrimp), shelled and de-veined
450g (16 oz) skinless, boneless
  chicken breast, cut into 5cm
  (2 in) pieces

For the guacamole
3 avocados, stoned and chopped
1 small red onion, diced
1 jalapeño chilli, deseeded
  and diced
2 garlic cloves, crushed
1 lime, juiced
small bunch of coriander
  (cilantro), leaves picked
  and chopped
small bunch of mint, leaves
  picked and chopped
200ml (1 cup) soured cream
sea salt and freshly ground
  black pepper

To serve
2 limes, cut into wedges

Put all the ingredients for the guacamole into a large bowl and mix everything together. Season to taste with salt and pepper.

Heat the vegetable oil in a deep-fat fryer to 160°C/325°F or in a deep heavy-based saucepan until a breadcrumb sizzles and turns brown when dropped into it. Note: hot oil can be dangerous; do not leave it unattended.

Mix the panko and almonds together in a large shallow bowl. Put the flour into a separate bowl and season well, then put the eggs into another separate bowl.

Cut the prawns (shrimp) in half. Dip all the prawns and chicken into the seasoned flour, dusting off any excess, then coat each piece first in the beaten egg, then in the almond mixture. Put on a large plate.

Line a large shallow dish with kitchen paper. Deep-fry the chicken in batches for 5–6 minutes, and the prawns for 3–4 minutes, until crisp and golden brown, then drain on the kitchen paper and season with salt.

Pile the deep-fried prawns and chicken onto a large platter and serve with the guacamole and lime wedges.

I made these rolls shortly after a few laps with racing legend Mario Andretti. At 77 he drives a car like he's nicked it – really fast! My stint in front of the cameras, overlooking the circuit and Sonoma, with Napa Valley beyond in the distance, was pretty memorable.

CALIFORNIA & SUSHI ROLLS

=== SERVES 4 ===

For the mayonnaise
1 medium egg yolk
1 teaspoon Dijon mustard
200ml (1 cup) vegetable oil
1 tablespoon yuzu juice
sea salt and freshly ground
   black pepper

For the rolls
4 sheets sushi nori
250g (1 cup) sushi rice, cooked
   according to pack instructions,
   adding 3 tablespoons rice
   vinegar after cooling
4 x 25g (1 oz) slices skinless fresh
   salmon, belly removed
1 avocado, stoned and thinly sliced
8 thin slices cucumber, without
   seeds, each around 5cm (2 in)
   in length
2 tablespoons chopped
   coriander (cilantro)
1 teaspoon black sesame seeds
1 teaspoon white sesame seeds
100g (3½ oz) cooked king
   crab meat

For the dip
5cm (2 in) piece fresh root ginger
2 tablespoons soy sauce
1 teaspoon toasted sesame oil

You will also need a sushi mat

For the mayo, whisk the egg yolk and mustard together in a bowl. Slowly add the oil, a drop at a time, and whisk continuously until the mixture starts to thicken and emulsify. Continue to whisk, pouring the oil in at a steady drizzle until it has all been added. Whisk in the yuzu and season. Spoon into a piping bag.

For the dip, grate the ginger into a bowl using a fine grater to extract all the ginger juice. Stir in the soy sauce and sesame oil.

To make the sushi rolls, place a sheet of nori onto a sushi mat. Spoon about a quarter of the rice on top then use wet fingertips to flatten the rice down and cover the nori in a thin flat layer, leaving a 1cm (½ in) border at the bottom and top of the sheet.

Lay half the salmon horizontally along the bottom edge of the rice. Top with a quarter of the avocado, half the cucumber and half the coriander (cilantro), pipe over the mayo and use the mat to wrap up and around the nori to roll it up tightly, wetting the edge of the nori sheet to help it stick down. Repeat with another nori sheet using the same quantity of rice, cucumber, avocado, coriander and the rest of the salmon.

For the California rolls, place a nori sheet on top of a board. Spoon half the remaining rice on top, and press down in a thin flat layer, leaving a border as before. Sprinkle over half the sesame seeds and cover the rice with a sheet of clingfilm (plastic wrap). Flip the whole thing over, including the clingfilm, onto the sushi mat. Place half the crab and half the remaining avocado at the bottom end of the rice, then roll up tightly, using the mat and clingfilm. Wet the edge of the nori and secure. Repeat with the last nori sheet and remaining ingredients. Slice the rolls into 6 pieces, trimming as necessary. Arrange on a plate and serve with the dip.

In California we visited The Shed, a restaurant combined with the ultimate cook shop, just down the road from the Single Thread, where our lunch was served on long wooden boards. Browsing the shop, I couldn't help myself, and bought a leather knife roll and a few Japanese knives.

CHICKEN WINGS
WITH QUINOA & AUBERGINE

=== SERVES 6 ===

800g (1¾ lb) chicken wings
8 baby aubergines (eggplants)
sea salt and freshly ground
  black pepper
4 tablespoons maple syrup
8 tablespoons olive oil,
  plus extra for drizzling
200g (1 cup) quinoa
2 red onions, cut into 8 wedges
2 regular aubergines (eggplants)
4 lemons
bunch of flat-leaf parsley,
  finely chopped
bunch of coriander
  (cilantro), finely chopped
bunch of mint, finely chopped
1 tablespoon white sesame seeds
1 tablespoon black sesame seeds
100g (3½ oz) walnuts, chopped
100g (¾ cup) feta cheese
1 eating apple, cut into julienne
small handful of micro herbs
  (optional)

Preheat the oven to 220°C/425°F/gas mark 7.

Place the chicken wings and baby aubergines (eggplants) in a large roasting tray, season and drizzle over the maple syrup and half the olive oil. Roast in the oven for 5 minutes.

Wash the quinoa in a sieve under cold running water and put into a medium pan. Pour in enough water to cover, put a lid on the pan and bring to the boil. Simmer for 20 minutes.

Put the onion wedges into the roasting tray and cook for a further 25 minutes.

Cut the regular aubergines in half lengthways, then cut in half again into strips. Place on a separate roasting tray, drizzle in oil and season. Roast for 20 minutes.

Place the cooked regular aubergines on a board and remove the stalks. Chop the flesh and put into a large food processor. Add the juice from 1 lemon and season. Add 4 tablespoons olive oil and blend for 2 minutes until smooth. Taste and adjust with more lemon juice and seasoning, if desired.

Drain the quinoa through a sieve and run under cold water then shake the sieve well to drain fully. Tip into a bowl and stir in the chopped herbs, the rest of the lemon juice, the sesame seeds and three-quarters of the walnuts. Season well.

To serve, spoon the puréed aubergine onto a large platter, top with the quinoa, then spoon over the chicken wings, onions and baby aubergines. Spoon the juices from the tray over the top. Crumble over the feta cheese, scatter over the apple and micro herbs (if using). Drizzle with olive oil, if desired.

The idea for this dish came when I was wandering around Los Angeles trying to find somewhere for lunch. With a cold beer in my hand, I was served this delicious flatbread, straight from the wood-fired oven. Here is the recipe – simple, easy and cheaper than a flight to Beverly Hills.

MACKEREL, BEET & FENNEL FLATBREAD

=== SERVES 6 ===

For the flatbread
375g (2⅔ cups) self-raising (self-rising) flour, plus extra for dusting
salt
1 tablespoon coriander seeds, crushed

For the topping
100g (½ cup) mascarpone
100g (½ cup) soft blue cheese
large handful of kale
12 small cooked beetroot (beets), sliced
2 red onions, cut into thin wedges
1 fennel, thinly sliced, reserving the fennel fronds
6 x 100g (3½ oz) mackerel fillets, pin bones removed
1 teaspoon coriander seeds
80ml (⅓ cup) olive oil
½ apple, cut into thin strips
a few sprigs of bergamot (optional)
freshly ground black pepper

Preheat the oven to 240°C/475°F/gas mark 9.

For the flatbread, put the flour into the bowl of a freestanding mixer fitted with a K beater. Add a pinch of salt, 1 tablespoon of water and the coriander seeds and mix for 1–2 minutes to make a dough. It should feel slightly tacky.

For the topping, mix together the mascarpone and blue cheese together in a bowl. Strip the kale from the stalks.

Flour a board and roll out the bread dough, transfer to a floured tray (around 60 x 30cm/24 x 12 in) and roll the dough until it is approximately 5mm (¼ in) thick. Dimple all over with your fingertips. If you don't have a large oven, divide the dough in half, roll out to the same thickness and transfer to two smaller floured baking trays.

Spread the cheese mixture all over the dough, top with the beetroot (beets), onion, fennel and kale.

Cut each mackerel fillet in half and place, skin-side up, on top of the vegetables, on the flatbread. Season with salt and pepper, sprinkle over the coriander seeds and drizzle over half the olive oil.

Bake in the preheated oven for 20 minutes, or in a pizza oven for 6–8 minutes.

To serve, scatter over the apple strips, fennel fronds and bergamot leaves (if using), then drizzle with the remaining olive oil.

The first time I had deep-fried soft-shell crab was at Wolfgang Puck's famous restaurant Spago in Beverly Hills. Many people claim to be successful chefs but this guy has taken it to another level. Known as 'Mr Beverly Hills', Wolfgang was one of a small group of cooks that first put American food on the world stage. As well as being a good friend and a top-class cook, he is also a top-class entertainer.

DEEP-FRIED INDIAN SOFT-SHELL CRAB
WITH MANGO SAUCE

=== SERVES 6 ===

For the crab
1 litre (5 cups) vegetable oil, for deep-frying
75g (½ cup) cornflour (cornstarch)
2 tablespoons medium curry powder
1 tablespoon black onion seeds
2 medium eggs, beaten
6 small soft-shell crabs

For the mango sauce
75g (¾ cup) cream cheese
½ large mango, peeled and diced
2 tablespoons chopped coriander (cilantro)
2 tablespoons chopped mint
2 limes, zested and juiced
sea salt and freshly ground black pepper

To garnish
Hoja Santa leaves (optional)
pea shoots, micro coriander (cilantro) and borage flowers (optional)
1 tablespoon coconut shreds or flakes
1 lime, cut into 6 wedges

Make the mango sauce. Spoon the cream cheese into a medium bowl and add the mango, chopped herbs, lime zest and juice and mix everything together. Season to taste.

Heat the vegetable oil in a deep-fat fryer to 200°C/400°F or in a deep heavy-based saucepan until a breadcrumb sizzles and turns brown when dropped into it. Note: hot oil can be dangerous; do not leave it unattended.

Mix the cornflour (cornstarch), curry powder and onion seeds together in a bowl and season. Put the beaten eggs into a medium bowl. Line a large dish with kitchen paper.

Dip the soft-shell crabs first into the beaten eggs, then into the flour mixture shaking off any excess. Deep-fry the crab, two at a time, for 2–3 minutes, then lift out and drain on the kitchen paper. Season with salt.

Spread the Hoja Santa leaves (if using) over a large plate then spoon the mango sauce on top. Pile up the crabs then sprinkle over the pea shoots, micro coriander (cilantro), borage flowers (if using) and coconut. Serve with the lime wedges on the side.

To be brutally honest I am not built for Speedos and the day we spent at Muscle Beach in Santa Monica, you could definitely spot me – the only Brit – in my shoes, socks, trousers and a shirt! So while the gods and goddesses paraded around me wearing little more than a loin cloth, I took inspiration from the Santa Monica farmer's market, with the help of Rapheal Lunetta (who's kind of famous for cooking in these parts). The market was spectacular, full of amazing locally grown produce, including ginger on the stem, which was about five foot long!

JAPANESE BROTH
WITH SEA BASS, LOBSTER & TOFU

SERVES 4

1 tablespooon white miso paste
750ml (3 cups) water
10cm (4 in) piece fresh root ginger, peeled and cut into 4 pieces
1 lemongrass stalk, halved lengthways
3 sheets dried kombu seaweed
2 tablespoons mirin
4 tablespoons soy sauce
200g (7 oz) enoki mushrooms
100g (3½ oz) oyster mushrooms
2 black radishes or 50g (1¾ oz) mooli
1 small bunch Tenderstem broccoli
2 pak choi (bok choy), halved lengthways
2 sea bass, halved to make 4 fillets
2 lobster tails, halved lengthways
300g (10½ oz) tofu
small bunch of Vietnamese coriander (cilantro) or coriander, leaves picked

In a bowl, mix together the miso paste with 200ml (1 cup) of the water to make a paste. Pour the rest of the water into a large pan and bring to the boil. Stir in the paste to dissolve.

Add the ginger and lemongrass to the stock with the kombu seaweed and pour in the mirin and soy sauce.

Bring the broth to the boil, then lift the kombu out with a slotted spoon. Drop in the mushrooms, radishes, broccoli, pak choi (bok choy), sea bass and lobster, the tofu, and the coriander (cilantro) leaves.

Cover the pan with a lid, reduce the heat to a simmer and cook for 8 minutes.

Taste the broth to check the seasoning and add a splash or two more of soy sauce, if desired. Ladle into bowls and serve.

Fort Worth is a Texan cattle-ranch town, with all the old buildings still intact. It's a popular tourist destination, and is almost like Disneyland for cows. Instead of Mickey Mouse and Pluto, you see cowboys and longhorn cattle wandering the streets. With rodeo stadiums everywhere you look, it's a good place to visit.

FORT WORTH CHICKEN WINGS
WITH ORANGE & SLAW

=== SERVES 4 ===

vegetable oil, for deep-frying
75g (½ cup) cornflour (cornstarch)
sea salt and freshly ground
   black pepper
900g (2 lb) chicken wings

For the slaw
2 medium egg yolks
1 teaspoon Dijon mustard
200ml (1 cup) olive oil
2 teaspoons grainy mustard
1 celeriac (celery root), peeled
   and thinly sliced into batons
1 apple, cored and thinly
   sliced into batons

For the sauce
100ml (½ cup) maple syrup
2 tablespoons sherry vinegar
2 jalapeño chillies, chopped
6 spring onions (scallions),
   trimmed and sliced
zest and juice of 1 orange

First make the slaw. Put the egg yolks and mustard into a medium bowl and whisk together. Slowly add the oil, starting with a drop at a time, and whisk continuously until the mixture starts to thicken and emulsify. Continue to whisk, pouring the oil in at a steady drizzle now until all the oil has been added. Stir in the grainy mustard and season to taste. Fold in the celeriac (celery root) and apple and spoon into a serving bowl.

Heat the vegetable oil in a deep-fat fryer to 160°C/325°F or in a deep heavy-based saucepan until a breadcrumb sizzles and turns brown when dropped into it. Note: hot oil can be dangerous; do not leave it unattended. Line a large plate with kitchen paper.

Put the cornflour (cornstarch) into a medium shallow dish and season with the salt and pepper. Dip each chicken wing in to coat in the seasoned flour, then deep-fry in batches for 8–10 minutes until golden and crisp. Drain on the kitchen paper and sprinkle with salt.

Place all the ingredients for the sauce into a large frying pan and place over a medium heat. Bring to the boil, then simmer until the sauce has reduced by about a third. Put the wings into the frying pan in 2–3 batches and spoon over the sauce to coat them. Bubble over a low heat for 2 minutes to heat the chicken through.

To serve, spoon the wings and sauce onto a large warm platter and serve with the slaw.

This is my favourite way to eat a hot dog. These have to be made with packet or tinned hot dogs (not fancy ones!), and are inspired by the Corny Dogs I tried at the Texas State Fair. The stand opens solely for the fair, and sells hundreds of thousands of Corny Dogs. A sausage-on-a-stick coated in cornmeal and deep-fried – like a savoury lollipop!

ULTIMATE HOT DOG
WITH SLOPPY

=== SERVES 4 ===

8 hot dog sausages
4 brioche hot dog buns

For the sauce
2 tablespoons olive oil,
   plus extra for frying
1 onion, finely diced
4 garlic cloves, chopped
1 red pepper, finely diced
400g (14 oz) minced
   (ground) beef
2 tablespoons tomato purée
2 tablespoons harissa
1 tablespoon chipotle chilli
4 tablespoons soy sauce
200ml (1 cup) tomato ketchup
1 bay leaf
a few sprigs of rosemary
sea salt and freshly ground
   black pepper
small bunch of coriander
   (cilantro), chopped, plus
   a few sprigs for garnish

For the onion rings
vegetable oil, for deep-frying
100g (¾ cup) plain
   (all-purpose) flour
235ml (1 cup) milk
1 onion

First make the sauce. Heat the oil in a large pan and add the onion, garlic and pepper. Stir everything together and cook over a low to medium heat for 10 minutes. Stir in the mince and brown in the pan for about 10–15 minutes until golden.

Add the tomato purée to the pan, followed by the harissa, chipotle chilli, soy sauce, tomato ketchup, bay and rosemary. Season well and stir everything together, then bring the sauce to a gentle simmer and cook for 15 minutes. Add 4 tablespoons more soy or water, if desired.

To make the onion rings, first heat the vegetable oil in a deep-fat fryer to 200°C/400°F or in a deep heavy-based saucepan until a breadcrumb sizzles and turns brown when dropped into it. Note: hot oil can be dangerous; do not leave it unattended.

Put the flour into a bowl and season well. Pour the milk into a separate bowl. Slice the onions into rounds, then drop a handful into the milk, lift out and place into the bowl of seasoned flour. Do the same until all the onion is coated in the flour.

Deep-fry the onion rings in batches for 2 minutes until golden, then drain on kitchen paper and sprinkle with salt.

Heat a drizzle of oil in a non-stick frying pan. Add the hot dogs to the pan, along with 4 tablespoons of water and steam-fry until warmed through. Drain.

Stir the coriander (cilantro) into the mince sauce and check the seasoning. Split the buns, fill each one with two hot dogs, spoon over the sauce and top with onion rings and coriander sprigs.

We cooked these in the grounds of Houmas House, an old Louisiana plantation. The gardens were extremely impressive, with some of the most beautiful trees I've ever seen, although the house itself has a somewhat dark and mysterious past. There is no question it is a beautiful spot though, right on the banks of the Mississippi, hence the shrimp.
If you visit, don't forget to book onto the ghost tour with Susan!

SHRIMP HUSH PUPPIES

SERVES 6

1 litre (5 cups) vegetable oil, for deep-frying
1kg (2¼ lb) raw prawns (shrimp), head on, peeled and de-veined
sea salt

For the hush puppy batter
2 medium eggs
85g (about ⅔ cup) cornmeal
45g (⅓ cup) plain (all-purpose) flour
1 teaspoon caster (superfine) sugar
1 teaspoon baking powder
1 teaspoon bicarbonate of soda (baking soda)
1 teaspoon sea salt
1 teaspoon freshly ground black pepper
2 tablespoons creamed corn
100ml (½ cup) buttermilk
1 small onion, chopped
1 jalapeño chilli, chopped
200g (2 cups) grated Cheddar cheese

To serve
spicy dip, such as Sriracha
1 lemon, cut into wedges
1 lime, cut into wedges

To make the hush puppy batter, put one of the eggs into a bowl and beat well. Set aside.

Put the other egg into a separate large bowl, beat well, then add the remaining batter ingredients. Mix everything together well.

Heat the vegetable oil in a deep-fat fryer to 180°C/350°F or in a deep heavy-based saucepan until a breadcrumb sizzles and turns brown when dropped into it. Note: hot oil can be dangerous; do not leave it unattended.

Line a large plate with kitchen paper. Dip each prawn (shrimp) first in the beaten egg until coated, then into the hush puppy batter, to coat. Deep-fry in the oil in batches, four prawns at a time, for 3 minutes until golden brown and crisp. Lift out and drain on the kitchen paper. Season with salt.

Spoon the spicy dip into a small bowl, arrange the prawns on a platter and serve with the lemon and lime wedges to squeeze over.

Wherever you go food shopping in the States, there will always be plenty of corn on offer. Simple to make, this dish uses the sweetest corn on the husk. You can also make it with tinned sweetcorn, if you like.

CRAB & CORN SOUP
WITH FRITTERS

=== SERVES 4 ===

For the soup
2 tablespoons butter
½ white onion, finely diced
1 green (bell) pepper, finely diced
2 celery sticks, finely diced
1 tablespoon plain
   (all-purpose) flour
6 tablespoons white wine
500ml (2 cups) hot chicken stock
100ml (½ cup) double
   (heavy) cream
sea salt and freshly ground
   black pepper
1 corn on the cob, kernels
   removed
200g (7 oz) white crab meat
5cm (2 in) piece fresh root ginger,
   peeled and finely diced
1 lime, juiced

For the fritters
200g (1½ cups) plain
   (all-purpose) flour
1 tablespoon baking powder
2 medium eggs
200ml (1 cup) milk
1 corn on the cob,
   kernels removed
100g (3½ oz) white crab meat
2 tablespoons flat-leaf
   parsley, chopped
4 tablespoons butter

To garnish
edible flowers and spring onion
   (scallion) tops, thinly sliced
good-flavoured olive oil

To make the soup, put the butter into a large saucepan and place over a medium heat. Once the butter has melted and is foaming, stir in the onion, pepper and celery. Lower the heat slightly and cook for a few minutes, stirring occasionally and not letting the vegetables colour, then stir in the flour. Cook for a few more minutes to cook out the flour. Next, pour the wine into the pan, bring to a bubble, then stir in the stock. Turn up the heat slightly so that the liquid comes to the boil, then add the cream. Season, then reduce the heat to a simmer and cook gently for 5 minutes.

Meanwhile, make the fritters. In a large bowl, mix together the flour, baking powder and eggs. Slowly add the milk and keep stirring so that the mixture forms a thick batter. It should be dropping consistency – to check, lift the spoon up and allow a dollop of the mixture to drop back into the mix. It should fall after a slight pause. Add the corn kernels, crab meat and parsley, season with salt and pepper and fold everything together.

Heat a large frying pan over a medium heat, add a tablespoon of butter and once the butter has melted and is foaming, place three large spoonfuls of the batter into the pan, well-spaced apart. Cook for 1–2 minutes until golden brown, then flip over and cook for a further 1–2 minutes. Lift onto a plate and repeat three more times until all the batter has been used up and you've made 12 fritters.

Stir the soup to check the consistency (it should be fairly thick), then stir in the corn, crab, ginger, lime juice and taste to check the seasoning. Ladle the soup into bowls and sprinkle over the edible flowers and spring onion (scallion) tops. Drizzle with olive oil and serve with the fritters.

I've cooked in some peculiar places, but on a floating platform in the middle of a massive swamp is a new one on me. Not only was it 120 degrees in Lafayette, but the crew boat cleared off and left me on my own for an hour! The last thing the tour guide said as he disappeared around the corner was that there were four thousand alligators in the water so it was wise not to throw any scraps or rubbish off the platform!

SHRIMP-WRAPPED BACON & OYSTERS

⟹ SERVES 6 ⟹

12 oysters, shucked, reserving the
   juices and the rounded shells
handful of collard greens or
   spring greens, finely shredded
12 large raw prawns (shrimp),
   peeled
100g (3½ oz) cooked white
   crab meat
1 tablespoon Old Bay Seasoning
6 slices streaky bacon, halved
½ eating apple, cut into julienne
small handful of micro herbs
   (optional)
1 lemon, juiced

For the sauce
4 tablespoons Sriracha
4 tablespoons honey
½ green pepper (bell pepper),
   deseeded and finely diced
2 lemons, juiced
sea salt and freshly ground
   black pepper

Preheat the barbecue: when the coals are silvery in colour, it's ready.

Put all the ingredients for the sauce in a small pan, season well and stir together.

Fill the rounded shells from the oysters with the shredded collards, then top each with an oyster and some of the juices. Spoon over some of the sauce and place them directly on the coals, and cook for 5 minutes.

Meanwhile, put the pan with the sauce in it on the barbecue to warm through, stirring occasionally.

To cook the prawns (shrimp), cut about two-thirds of the way through the back of each one. Take out the vein and discard. Use a teaspoon to fill with crab meat and season with the Old Bay. Wrap each prawn tightly in a strip of bacon and pop onto the barbecue. Cook for 5 minutes, turning halfway through.

Lift the prawns onto a large platter, along with the oysters, and drizzle over any remaining sauce. Pour over the lemon juice and sprinkle over the apple and micro herbs (if using), to serve.

Roasted in the oven is one of the best ways to eat avocado, and an absolute must when talking about Californian food. Forget slathering it all over your face as a beauty treatment; instead fill avocado halves with lime butter and stick them in the oven. These are also great roasted on a barbecue, skins on, and wrapped in tin foil.

CHICKEN WINGS & AVOCADO
ROASTED IN A CHILLI, LIME, MINT & MAPLE SYRUP BUTTER

SERVES 6

2 shallots, chopped
3 garlic cloves
3 red chillies, roughly chopped
small bunch of mint
500g (2 cups) butter
3 limes, zested and juiced
8 tablespoons maple syrup
6 avocados with skin, halved and stoned
6 baby aubergines (eggplants)
500g (1 lb 2 oz) chicken wings
sea salt and freshly ground black pepper

Preheat the oven to 220°C/425°F/gas mark 7.

Put the shallots, garlic and chillies into a large food processer. Blitz for about 20 seconds then add the mint, blitz again to combine, then add the butter and lime zest. Blitz again for another 20–30 seconds, then pour in the maple syrup. Keep mixing to whip the butter for a further minute or two.

Place the avocados into a large roasting tray with the baby aubergines (eggplants). Top with the chicken wings, season and dot over the butter. Roast in the preheated oven for 30–40 minutes, or in a pizza oven for 15 minutes.

Pour over the lime juice and serve the chicken straight from the roasting tray.

You may think that using ready-made ingredients is cheating, but looking around us at the yachts in The Hamptons, it seemed to make sense.

LOBSTER & MANGO IN A MARINA

SERVES 2

100ml (½ cup) olive oil, plus extra for frying
30g (1 oz) wild rice
8 small pickled onions, drained and halved
150g (⅔ cup) butter
12 baby carrots
2 cooked lobsters
2 medium eggs, beaten
4 tablespoons panko breadcrumbs
2 crostini
100ml (½ cup) mayonnaise
2 tablespoons ready-made mango chilli sauce, plus extra to serve

For the salsa
100g (3½ oz) fresh mango, diced
1 tablespoon diced dried mango
1 tablespoon dried cranberries, diced
1 tablespoon ready-made mango chilli sauce
sea salt and freshly ground black pepper

To garnish
endive leaves, frisée lettuce and micro herbs (optional)
balsamic vinegar

Make the salsa. Mix all the ingredients in a bowl, and season.

Heat the olive oil in a large non-stick frying pan to 160°C/325°F and fry the wild rice for 30 seconds. Drain on kitchen paper.

Discard the oil, then return the pan to the hob over a medium heat. Fry the onions, flat-side down, until charred, then drain on kitchen paper. Put the butter into the same pan and melt over a medium heat until bubbling. Add the carrots, cook for 2 minutes, lift out and drain on the kitchen paper. Keep the butter to one side.

Cut off the head of the lobster with a sharp knife, set aside. Extract the meat from the body: use sharp scissors to cut between the under belly shell and the outer shells on both sides, then pull the strip away. Pull out the meat. Trim the tail from the body into a 5cm (2 in) piece. Set aside. Remove the knuckles from the head part of the shell and use a skewer to extract the meat. Wiggle the small claw to break it off from the large claw. Pull out and remove the shell inside with the meat clinging to it. Take off the meat. Use the back of a knife to crack both sides of the larger claw. Remove and discard the shell. You should be left with one whole body, two claws and extra meat. Repeat with the other lobster.

Put the eggs in a bowl and the breadcrumbs in another. Dip the claws in the egg then the breadcrumbs. Heat a little oil in a frying pan and shallow fry for 1–2 minutes until crispy. Cut each piece of lobster body meat into three.

Spoon a quenelle of mango salsa onto the crostini. Mix the mayonnaise in a bowl with the mango chilli sauce.

To serve, spread the mayo mixture over a platter, shaping it in an 'S' shape. Pop the lobster head at the top and tail at the bottom, arrange the rest of the lobster on top of the mayo with the crostini. Top with the carrots, lettuce, rice and onions. Drizzle over the balsamic vinegar and extra mango chilli sauce before serving.

Invented by a hot dog guy for a taxi diver who wanted to grab something quick to eat, the Philly cheesesteak has become massive in its home city of Philadelphia. Its fame has come at a price, however, and unfortunately it is now easier to find a bad one than a tasty one. This has to be made with great beef, normally rib-eye, cooked quickly then sliced up. Provolone cheese is another must. Other than the hoagie – the type of bread it sits in – the rest is up to you.

PHILLY CHEESESTEAK

═══ SERVES 3 ═══

4 tablespoons olive oil
3 x 20cm (8 in) hoagies or
  baguettes, cut in half lengthways
6 large spring onions (scallions),
  cut in half lengthways
2 little gem lettuces, leaves
  pulled apart
50g (1¾ oz) cherry tomatoes
500g (1 lb 2 oz) rib-eye steak,
  thinly sliced
3 pickled onions, sliced
2 mozzarella balls, torn
300g (3 cups) grated
  provolone cheese

Preheat the oven to 200°C/400°F/gas mark 6. Heat a griddle pan to hot.

Drizzle the oil over the cut sides of the baguettes and place cut-side down onto the griddle. Toast until charred. Brush a little oil over the spring onions (scallions) and griddle them for 2–3 minutes, again until charred.

Place the baguettes in a parcel of foil or baking parchment, top with the lettuce and tomatoes.

Oil the griddle and place the steak on the griddle to cook for 1 minute on each side. Then cut up in to strips while on the griddle.

Place the strips of steak into the baguettes. Add the slices of pickled onion, mozzarella, provolone cheese, and top with the spring onions. Place in the oven for 5 minutes before serving.

This stuffed, layered sandwich has taken Louisiana by storm. Created in 1906 at a grocery store in New Orleans, where it was popular with Italian immigrants, a muffalata is made from salami or ham, pickles and provolone cheese with Sicilian-style bread.

MUFFALATA WITH SLAW

SERVES 6

1 round loaf of crusty bread, around 400g (14 oz)
100g (3½ oz) sliced ham
100g (3½ oz) provolone cheese, sliced
100g (3½ oz) sliced salami
100g (3½ oz) pimento-stuffed green olives, sliced
2 x 125g (4½ oz) mozzarella balls, sliced
2 tablespoons butter, at room temperature

For the pickle
100g (½ cup) caster (superfine) sugar
100ml (½ cup) white wine vinegar
2 carrots
¼ romanesco cauliflower, shredded
½ red onion, diced

For the slaw
2 tablespoons soy sauce
2 tablespoons runny honey
½ red cabbage, thinly sliced
½ red onion, diced
1 corn on the cob, kernels removed
1 tablespoon white sesame seeds
1 tablespoon black sesame seeds
½ teaspoon chilli flakes
sea salt and freshly ground black pepper

Put the loaf of bread on a board and cut a circle from the top, 20cm (8in) wide and around 3cm (1 in) deep. Set aside, take all the bread out of the middle of the loaf (save this to make breadcrumbs and then freeze).

To make the pickle, put the sugar and vinegar into a medium saucepan and bring to the boil. Using a potato peeler, peel ribbons off the carrots and put into a large bowl. Add the shredded cauliflower and diced red onion, then pour over the liquid and set aside to cool.

For the slaw, whisk the soy sauce and honey together in a large bowl, then add the remaining slaw ingredients, season and mix well.

Layer the ham, provolone cheese, salami, mozzarella, olives and pickle inside the hollowed-out loaf, seasoning between each layer. Repeat until the bread is filled up, then press down with your hands. Pop the bread lid on top.

Slice the loaf into six slices. Take a piece of foil large enough to wrap around a sandwich slice and brush butter all over it. Wrap a slice in the foil to make a parcel. Do the same with all the other slices.

Heat a large frying pan until hot and fry a couple of parcels at once, for 3–4 minutes until the cheese is bubbling. Unwrap each parcel and serve with a spoonful of the slaw.

FISH

We visited a wonderful farm just a stone's throw away from the sea and Santa Cruz. As we arrived, the sun burnt off the sea mist to reveal acres upon acres of artichokes, corn and soft fruit lining the road. The farm also had an amazing family-run shop. If you are ever in the area, pay them a visit. This dish is a combination of snapper from the sea and artichokes from the land. It is simple to prepare, and simple to cook.

ARTICHOKES, BEANS & EARLY GIRL TOMATO RAGOUT WITH SNAPPER

=== SERVES 2 ===

For the snapper
1 teaspoon olive oil,
  plus extra for drizzling
2 x 125g (4½ oz) red
  snapper fillets
sea salt and freshly ground
  black pepper

For the ragout
4 large artichokes
½ lemon, sliced
6 tablespoons olive oil
½ white onion, diced
3 garlic cloves, chopped
400g (14 oz) Early Girl
  tomatoes or on-the-vine
  tomatoes, quartered
150g (5¼ oz) fresh green beans,
  trimmed and chopped into
  5cm (2 in) pieces
large handful of baby leaf
  spinach, washed
handful of rocket
  (arugula) leaves

To prepare the artichokes for the ragout, cut the top off each artichoke, about halfway through the middle, and trim the stalk at the base. Take off all the leaves and use a spoon to scrape out the choke. Discard both the leaves and the hairy choke. Use a vegetable peeler to strip away the tough outer peel of each artichoke heart. Fill a medium bowl with cold water and add the lemon slices and the artichoke hearts and put to one side.

Place a medium heavy-based frying pan over a medium heat and drizzle in 1 teaspoon olive oil for the fish. When the oil is hot, add the snapper to the pan, skin-side down, and season well with salt and pepper. Cook for 3 minutes, then flip the fillets over. Carefully lift onto a warm plate.

In the same pan, pour in 6 tablespoons olive oil and heat over a medium heat. Stir in the onion and garlic, fry for 1 minute, then add the tomatoes and beans. Stir everything again, then cover the pan with a lid. Turn the heat down and simmer for 5 minutes.

Lift the artichoke hearts out of the water and chop each one on a board into four or five slices. Add to the pan with the tomato and beans. Cook gently for a further 2–3 minutes.

To finish, stir the spinach and rocket (arugula) into the pan, season with salt and pepper and place the fish on top. Drizzle with extra olive oil, if desired, then place the lid on the pan and cook for a further 2 minutes. Serve at once.

In my mind Thomas Keller is one of the greatest chefs in the world. He is the only chef in America to hold two Michelin 3-star restaurants, Per Se in New York and The French Laundry in Napa Valley, where I had the best meal of my life. I urge you to go there and try it for yourself. There was no way on earth that I was ever going to try and replicate anything from The French Laundry's extensive menu, but this dish was inspired by my time there.

MONKFISH & PRAWNS
WITH SQUID INK PINTO BEANS

SERVES 4

200g (1⅓ cups) dried pinto beans
2 tablespoons squid ink
butter, for frying
1 shallot, finely chopped
1 garlic clove, chopped
4 tablespoons white wine
100ml (½ cup) chicken stock
olive oil, for frying
600g (1 lb 5 oz) prepared
  monkfish tail, cut into 1cm
  (½ in) slices
8 prawns (shrimp), shelled
  and de-veined
sea salt and freshly ground
  black pepper
small bunch of flat-leaf
  parsley, chopped
25g (1 oz) Parmesan cheese,
  grated
½ lemon, juiced

To serve
nasturtium leaves and edible
  flowers (optional)

The night before, put the pinto beans into a large bowl and cover with plenty of cold water. Leave to soak overnight. The next day, drain well, then tip the beans into a large saucepan, cover with plenty of cold water and bring to the boil. Add half the squid ink, and place over a medium heat. Bring gently to the boil, then turn down the heat and simmer gently for 1 hour until tender. Drain.

Heat a knob of butter in a large, deep non-stick frying pan, and once melted, stir in the shallot and garlic. Sauté over a low to medium heat for 30 seconds. Add the beans, then pour the wine, stock and remaining squid ink into the pan and simmer gently for a few minutes.

In a separate frying pan, add a drizzle of oil and a knob of butter and place over a medium heat. Once the butter has melted, fry the monkfish and prawns (shrimp) for 2–3 minutes until opaque. Season well.

Add the parsley and Parmesan to the beans, then season.

Add another knob of butter to the fish, pour over the lemon juice. Shake the pan quickly to mix the juice into the butter.

To serve, spoon the beans among four plates and top with the monkfish and prawns. Scatter the nasturtium leaves and edible flowers over the fish (if using), and serve.

This is a native San Francisco fish stew, traditionally made by Italian fishermen using the leftover fish from the catch, that they couldn't or wouldn't sell at the piers along the San Fran harbour. As such, it can be made with any fish or shellfish you have, and tinned tomatoes are great for giving it flavour.

CIOPPINO

SERVES 4–6

100ml (½ cup) white wine
2 x 500g (18 fl oz) cartons passata classica
4 tablespoons olive oil
3 or 4 star anise
4 garlic cloves, chopped
1 cooked crab
5 scallops, cleaned
5 raw large prawns (shrimp), shell on
250g (9 oz) clams, cleaned
250g (9 oz) mussels, cleaned
500g (1 lb 2 oz) halibut, cut into 4 even-sized pieces
500g (1 lb 2 oz) salmon cut into 3 even-sized pieces
1 teaspoon caster (superfine) sugar
sea salt and freshly ground black pepper
small bunch of flat-leaf parsley, chopped
1 sourdough loaf, sliced

Pour the wine into a large saucepan and place over a medium heat. Bring the wine to the boil and as soon as it's bubbling, pour in the passata and half the olive oil. Add the star anise and garlic to the pan, too, and stir everything together. Simmer for 2–3 minutes.

Carefully add all the fish to the pan and sprinkle over the sugar. Stir everything together gently and season. Pop the lid on the pan and gently bubble over a low heat for 10 minutes.

Scatter with parsley and drizzle with the remaining olive oil. Serve immediately with the sourdough bread.

San Francisco is a multicultural city, with the second largest China Town in the US (and one of the biggest in the world). I made this dish on a Second World War battleship overlooking Alcatraz. With the Golden Gate Bridge behind us, this was one of the highlights of the first week of our travels.

SAN FRAN PRAWNS
& EGG FRIED RICE

=== SERVES 4 ===

For the salad
1 large carrot
6 tablespoons dark soy sauce
4 tablespoons caster
  (superfine) sugar
1 teaspoon Szechuan
  peppercorns, crushed
1 teaspoon chilli flakes
2 lemongrass, thinly sliced
small bunch of coriander
  (cilantro), chopped

For the prawns
1 litre (5 cups) vegetable oil,
  for deep-frying
50g (⅓ cup) cornflour (cornstarch)
1 teaspoon Szechuan
  peppercorns, crushed
2 oranges, 1 zested and
  both juiced
500g (1 lb 2 oz) raw tiger prawns
  (shrimp), shelled and de-veined
sea salt
½ lotus root, peeled and
  thinly sliced

For the egg fried rice
1 tablespoon vegetable oil
200g (7 oz) cooked basmati
  rice, chilled
1 medium egg, beaten
2 spring onions (scallions),
  trimmed and sliced
2 tablespoons freshly chopped
  coriander (cilantro)

For the salad, cut the carrot into long ribbons. Place the soy sauce, sugar, crushed peppercorns, chilli flakes and lemongrass in a pan and heat gently. Cook until the sugar has dissolved and the sauce is syrupy. Add the carrot and coriander (cilantro) and toss everything together.

For the prawns, heat the vegetable oil in a deep-fat fryer to 180°C/350°F or in a deep heavy-based saucepan until a breadcrumb sizzles and turns brown when dropped into it. Note: hot oil can be dangerous; do not leave it unattended.

Mix the cornflour (cornstarch), crushed peppercorns, orange zest and juice together in a bowl to make a paste. Dip the prawns into the mixture to coat each one, then deep-fry in batches for 30 seconds until crisp and golden brown, and drain on kitchen paper. Sprinkle with salt.

In the same oil, deep-fry the sliced lotus root for 1 minute until golden brown and drain on kitchen paper. Sprinkle with salt.

To make the egg fried rice, heat the oil in a non-stick wok, then add the rice. Stir-fry for 2–3 minutes until the rice has warmed through. Pour the egg into the pan and cook until crispy, stirring it into the rice as it cooks, then stir in the spring onions (scallions) and coriander.

To serve, spoon the rice onto a plate and top with the prawns, lotus crisps and salad.

I cooked this dish in the grounds of the Kendall-Jackson Vineyard.
The garden there is run by Tucker Taylor, ex-gardener of
The French Laundry, and it's a beautiful place.

SESAME TUNA
WITH MAPLE SYRUP, CHARRED CORN & MELON, & PICKLES

=== SERVES 2 ===

For the pickles
6 tablespoons cider vinegar
50g (¼ cup) caster (superfine)
    sugar
½ mooli radish, peeled
    and thinly sliced
½ turnip, peeled and
    thinly sliced
4 radishes, 2 quartered
    and 2 sliced
a few beetroot (beet) leaves

For the tuna
1 tablespoon white sesame seeds
1 tablespoon black sesame seeds
1 tablespoon olive oil
2 x 150g (5¼ oz) tuna steaks
sea salt and freshly ground
    black pepper
1 tablespoon maple syrup

For the charred corn and melon
1 corn on the cob, kernels
    removed
½ Gypsy pepper or green
    pepper (bell pepper), diced
½ jalapeño chilli, diced
50g (1¾ oz) melon balls
2 tablespoons maple syrup
nasturtium flowers and leaves,
    to garnish (optional)

Place the vinegar and sugar into a medium saucepan and bring to the boil over a medium heat to dissolve the sugar. Once the sugar has dissolved, add the mooli, turnip and radishes, then take the pan off the heat and add the beetroot leaves.

Spoon both types of sesame seeds onto a large plate and mix together. Oil the tuna steaks and season on each side. Heat a heavy-based medium frying pan. When the pan is hot, cook the steaks for 1–2 minutes on each side. Drizzle over the maple syrup, then press each steak into the sesame seeds, turning them over to coat each side.

Place the same frying pan over a high heat and char the corn and peppers. Stir through the chilli, the melon and maple syrup and season with salt and pepper.

Spoon the corn mixture onto a plate, slice the tuna and place on top, then spoon over the pickles and 1 teaspoon of the pickle juice. Scatter with the nasturtium flowers and leaves (if using), then serve.

I don't know whether it's a sign of getting old, but going to a bar to drink tequila is quite possibly last on my list of things to do. I am much happier cooking with it. This dish was cooked on a barbecue, all the way through on one side, with the salmon skin protecting the flesh.

BBQ TEQUILA SALMON
WITH JALAPEÑOS

═══ SERVES 8–10 ═══

1 dried chipotle chilli
1 red onion, finely diced
1 garlic clove, crushed
200ml (1 cup) tomato ketchup
2 tablespoons honey
2 tablespoons molasses
4 tablespoons maple sugar
   or light brown soft sugar
1 teaspoon English
   mustard powder
2 limes, zested and juiced
4 tablespoons tequila
6 tablespoons olive oil
1 side salmon, pin-boned and
   trimmed, approx. 1.5kg (3 lb)
sea salt and freshly ground
   black pepper
14 small orange and red
   peppers (bell peppers)
6 jalapeño chillies
2 avocados, stoned and sliced
small bunch of coriander
   (cilantro), leaves picked
   and chopped

To serve
1 lime, zested (optional)

The night before, put the dried chilli in a bowl of cold water and leave to soak overnight.

The next day, preheat the barbecue: when the coals are silvery in colour, it's ready. Drain the chipotle chilli and chop.

Put the onion into a medium heavy-based flameproof pan, then add the garlic, ketchup, honey, molasses, maple sugar, mustard powder, lime zest and juice and the tequila. Stir everything together, then place onto the rack of the barbecue and simmer until the sugar has dissolved. Do this on the hob over a medium heat if you don't have a flameproof pan.

Brush about a third of the oil over the skin side of the salmon and season. Place skin-side down onto the barbecue and cook for 15 minutes, basting with some of the sauce. Sprinkle over half the chopped chilli and stir the rest into the sauce.

Drizzle the orange and red peppers (bell peppers) and the jalapeños with the remaining oil, season and put onto the barbecue alongside the salmon and cook for 5–10 minutes until the skins have blistered and softened, turning halfway.

Spoon the remaining sauce over a large platter and top with the peppers and avocado. Lift the salmon onto a board and use a knife and fork to flake the salmon into large chunks. Place on top of the peppers and avocado and sprinkle over a little extra lime zest, if you like. Scatter with the coriander (cilantro) and serve.

This dish is almost like a Mexican Moules Marinières, flavoured with coriander and lime. The tequila needs to be burnt off before cooking the mussels otherwise it will be too strong. This idea for this came to me after meeting chef Johnny Hernandez, who made one of the most amazing dishes that I had ever seen. It involved a 12-foot pit of charcoal, a metal coffin on a chain and a cow's head roasted for 12 hours... and my god it tasted so good. These mussels are a little bit easier to prepare.

MEXICAN MUSSELS

=== SERVES 4 ===

1 tablespoon butter
1 onion, diced
2 garlic cloves, chopped
2 celery sticks, diced
2 green chillies, diced
4 tablespoons tequila
250ml (1 cup) double
  (heavy) cream
3 limes, zested and juiced
2 large bunches of coriander
  (cilantro), freshly chopped
small bunch of mint,
  freshly chopped
salt and freshly ground
  black pepper
1.5kg (3 lb) mussels, cleaned

Heat the butter in a large, non-stick casserole pan, and once it's melted, sweat the onion, garlic and celery over a low heat until softened but not coloured. Keep the heat really low so the vegetables don't burn. It'll take around 15 minutes. Add the chillies to the pan, stir in and cook for 2–3 minutes.

Pour in the tequila and light the pan to burn off the alcohol, then pour in the cream and stir in. Add the lime zest, followed by half the herbs and season, then stir everything together. As soon as the sauce is boiling, tip in the cleaned mussels, stir all the ingredients together and cover the pan with a lid. Bring to the boil and cook for 3–4 minutes.

Take the lid off the pan, then pour over the lime juice. Sprinkle over the rest of the herbs, toss everything together and serve straight away.

Grits are made from corn, which is ground into coarse meal then cooked. They are usually served for breakfast and originated from the South. If you are ever in Austin, Texas, whatever you do, don't call grits polenta. The locals will not be happy with you! The most important thing with grits is to add plenty of flavour. Butter is my favourite, and lots of it.

GRITS WITH SHRIMP & OCTOPUS

500g (1 lb 2 oz) raw whole prawns (shrimp)
150g (5¼ oz) white corn grits or white polenta
2 corn on the cob
200g (7 oz) mixed wild mushrooms
50g (1¾ oz) baby leaf spinach, washed
9 tablespoons butter
sea salt and freshly ground black pepper
2 thick slices bacon, cut into 1cm (½ in) cubes
200g (7 oz) cooked octopus, cut into 5cm (2 in) chunks
½ green pepper (bell pepper), diced
1 lemon, juiced

Peel the prawns (shrimp) then pull the heads off and put both heads and shells into a medium pan. De-vein the prawns and set aside on a plate.

Pour 600ml (2½ cups) water into the pan of prawn shells, cover with a lid and bring to the boil. Strain into a separate medium pan and stir in the grits or white polenta. Place the pan over a low heat and bring to a simmer. Simmer gently for 20 minutes, stirring occasionally.

Secure one corn on the cob with tongs and hold over an open flame to char it for 3–4 minutes. Alternatively, place under a grill (broiler), turning regularly. Do the same with the other corn on the cob. Take a sharp knife and cut along the length of the cob to remove the corn from the husk, turning as you go.

Add half the mushrooms to the pan of grits with half the charred corn, the spinach and 7 tablespoons of the butter. Season with salt and pepper and stir everything together. Simmer gently.

Melt the remaining butter in a large frying pan over a medium heat. Add the remaining mushrooms and corn, the prawns, the cubed bacon, the octopus and the diced pepper and fry for 3 minutes, tossing every now and then.

Spoon the grits between two plates and top with the prawn mixture. Drizzle over the lemon juice and serve.

The key to Cajun cooking is the spice blend. I made this on the balcony of a hotel in the heart of New Orleans. As the sun set, the music got louder. The city transforms into a completely different animal at night-time. The Cajun rub and the sauce will work with any fish, if you don't have snapper.

CAJUN SNAPPER FILLETS
WITH LIME BEURRE BLANC

≡ SERVES 4 ≡

4 x 125g (4½ oz) snapper fillets,
  scaled and pin-boned
1 corn on the cob
1 tablespoon olive oil

For the Cajun rub
1 tablespoon sea salt
2 tablespoons garlic salt
3 tablespoons onion salt
4 tablespoons paprika
1 tablespoon freshly ground
  black pepper
2 teaspoons cayenne pepper
1 teaspoon dried oregano
1 teaspoon dried thyme

For the lime beurre blanc
250g (1 cup plus 2 tablespoons)
  chilled unsalted butter, diced
1 large shallot or small red
  onion, diced
1 garlic clove, chopped
4 tablespoons white wine
1 lime, zested and juiced

Mix together all the spices for the Cajun rub. Now put a few tablespoons of it into a shallow dish. Add the snapper fillets and rub the mixed spices all over the fish to coat.

Rest the corn on the cob on a board and use a sharp knife to slice the corn off the cob.

Place a large non-stick frying pan over a medium heat. Add the oil and a knob of butter (use a knob from the sauce) and allow to melt. When the butter is foaming, pop the fish in, hold it down to stop it curling and add the corn to the pan, alongside the fish. Cook for 4–5 minutes, flip the fish over and take the pan off the heat.

Meanwhile, put the shallot (or red onion), garlic and wine into a medium saucepan and bring to the boil. Simmer the mixture until the liquid has reduced by half. Turn the heat down to very low and slowly whisk in the cold butter, a little at a time, whisking well between each addition to make a thick sauce. Whisk in the lime zest and juice. Take the pan off the heat and pass the sauce through a fine sieve into a bowl. Keep the bowl in a warm place (not hot) and discard what's left in the sieve.

To serve, spoon the corn into the centre of four plates, top with the fish and spoon the sauce all around.

JAMES' TIP
You will have lots of Cajun rub left over. This can be stored in an airtight jar in the cupboard.

Wherever you go in New Orleans, you are surrounded by food and music.
I made this dish right in the heart of the city, in Louis Armstrong Park –
the perfect setting. The Creole flavours come from the French and
Spanish settlers that made Louisiana their home.

CREOLE-STYLE SHRIMP

≡ SERVES 4 ≡

2 tablespoons olive oil,
  plus extra for drizzling
8 slices crusty bread
1 knob of butter
1 medium onion, chopped
3 garlic cloves, chopped
1 tablespoon Creole seasoning
½ teaspoon cumin seeds
2 teaspoons dried thyme
6 tablespoons white wine
2 tablespoons tomato purée
2 x 400g (14 oz) tins
  chopped tomatoes
3 bay leaves
1 teaspoon caster (superfine)
  sugar
150g (5¼ oz) pimento-stuffed
  olives in brine, drained
2 tablespoons Worcestershire
  sauce
1 teaspoon hot sauce
sea salt and freshly ground
  black pepper
1kg (2¼ lb) raw prawns (shrimp),
  peeled and de-veined
small bunch of flat-leaf
  parsley, chopped
small bunch of basil, chopped

Heat 1 tablespoon of olive oil in a large non-stick frying pan over
a medium heat. Fry the bread slices in two batches until golden
and crispy, then lift onto a plate and put to one side.

In the same pan, add the remaining oil and the butter.
When the butter has melted and is bubbling, stir in the onion
and garlic and cook over a low heat for 2 minutes.

Put the Creole seasoning, cumin and thyme into a small
bowl. Add a splash of the white wine and stir in to make a paste.
Spoon into the pan with the onion and stir in.

Next, add the tomato purée, chopped tomatoes, bay leaves,
sugar, olives, Worcestershire sauce, hot sauce and the rest of
the wine. Season well and stir everything together then simmer
over a gentle heat for 5 minutes. Add the prawns (shrimp),
stir in and cook gently for a further 8 minutes.

Stir through the fresh herbs and taste to check the seasoning.
Remove the bay leaves. Drizzle over a little extra olive oil, if
desired, then spoon among four shallow bowls. Serve with
the toasted bread.

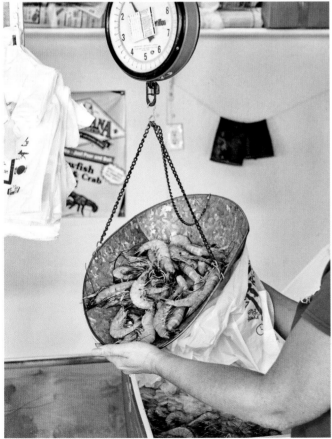

Louisiana has many famous dishes, from Beignets to Po' Boys. This is perhaps less well-known, but is still a classic. I had some of the best crab I have ever tasted in New Orleans, including beautiful blue crabs – feisty little things when you are trying to put them in a bag! I found the crab for this dish at Westwego, an amazing fish market by the side of the freeway. It had a stunning array of fresh seafood (as well as alligator!) from the waters and swampland surrounding New Orleans. Inspired by a French Gratin Dauphinois, the addition of Creole seasoning lightly flavours the crab meat in this delicious gratin.

CRAB & ALMOND GRATIN

=== SERVES 6 ===

1 tablespoon paprika
4 teaspoons dried thyme
4 teaspoons dried oregano
4 teaspoons celery salt
1 tablespoon ground
    white pepper
1kg (2¼ lb) white potatoes,
    thinly sliced
8 spring onions (scallions),
    chopped
100g (3½ oz) flaked
    (slivered) almonds
600g (1 lb 5 oz) white
    crab meat
few sprigs of thyme,
    leaves picked
500ml (2 cups) double
    (heavy) cream
2 tablespoons Dijon mustard
1 teaspoon Tabasco
25g (1 oz) Parmesan
    cheese, grated
100g (3½ oz) Cheddar
    cheese, grated

Preheat the oven to 180°C/350°F/gas mark 4.

Put all the herbs and spices, including the white pepper, into a small bowl and mix together.

Layer up the potatoes, spring onions (scallions), almonds and crab meat in a 1-litre (34-fl oz) casserole dish or ovenproof frying pan. Sprinkle the spice mix over each layer. Repeat until all the ingredients are used up, finishing with the fresh thyme then potatoes on top.

In a large bowl, whisk together the double (heavy) cream, mustard and Tabasco, then spoon over the top of the gratin.

Scatter the Parmesan and Cheddar over the top and bake for 45 minutes to 1 hour until golden and bubbling.

Redfish is a staple around Louisiana and the Mississippi River. It can be fried, grilled or barbecued and goes well with most sauces and garnishes. Use snapper or red mullet to get the same effect.

BBQ REDFISH & SOFT-SHELL CRAB
WITH GREEN TOMATOES & HERB SALSA

≡ SERVES 4 ≡

1 banana leaf
1kg (2¼ lb) redfish or red snapper, trimmed and gutted
200g (7 oz) white crab meat
1 lemon, sliced
sea salt and freshly ground black pepper
4 soft-shell crabs
2 large green tomatoes, thickly sliced

For the herb salsa
small bunch of flat-leaf parsley
small bunch of coriander (cilantro)
6 tablespoons olive oil
2 tablespoons white wine vinegar
1 large shallot or small red onion, diced
1 jalapeño chilli, diced
1 lemon, juiced

You will also need some food-safe string

Preheat the barbecue: when the coals are silvery in colour, it's ready. Lay the banana leaf on the rack of the barbecue for 1 minute to soften it. Set aside to cool.

Stuff the inside of the redfish with the crab meat, lemon slices and a quarter of the herbs from the salsa. Season well. Lay the fish on top of the banana leaf, wrap it round the fish then tie up with string so the filling is secure inside.

Lift onto the rack of the barbecue and cook for 15 minutes.

Season the soft-shell crabs and tomatoes, drizzle with a little of the oil from the salsa and place both on the barbecue. Cook for 15 minutes.

Meanwhile, chop the remaining herbs and put in a large bowl. Add the remaining oil, the vinegar, the shallot (or red onion), the diced jalapeño and the lemon juice and season well. Mix everything together.

Snip the string off the parcel of redfish and unwrap it, then place on a large platter with the soft-shell crab and tomatoes. Spoon over the herb salsa and serve.

This is my version of a Po' Boy – an open sandwich from Louisiana.
The clams in the local market were off the scale, about the size of tennis balls.

CLAM ROLLS
& BOSTON BAKED BEANS

=== SERVES 3 ===

20 large clams
1 litre (5 cups) vegetable oil,
    for deep-frying
125ml (½ cup) evaporated milk
100g (¾ cup) plain
    (all-purpose) flour
100g (¾ cup) fine cornmeal

For the tartare sauce
2 medium egg yolks
1 teaspoon Dijon mustard
200ml (1 cup) olive oil
½ lemon, juiced
1 tablespoon capers, chopped
3 cornichons, chopped
6 baby pearl onions, finely diced
small bunch of flat-leaf
    parsley, chopped
small bunch of dill, chopped
sea salt and freshly ground
    black pepper

For the Boston baked beans
200g (7 oz) piece bacon
2 tablespoons butter
2 tablespoons olive oil
100g (3½ oz) baby pearl onions
1 tablespoon dark brown sugar
2 tablespoons molasses
1 teaspoon English mustard
    powder
2 x 400g (14 oz) tins haricot
    (navy) beans, drained
small bunch of flat-leaf
    parsley, chopped

To serve
3 hot dog brioche buns
9 little gem lettuce leaves

Put the bacon piece into a saucepan, cover with cold water and bring to the boil. Reduce the heat and simmer for 45 minutes. Lift the bacon out of the liquid and cool, reserving the cooking liquor.

Make the tartare sauce. Whisk the egg yolks and mustard together in a bowl. Slowly add the oil, starting with a drop at a time, and whisk continuously until the mixture starts to thicken and emulsify. Continue to whisk, pouring the oil in at a steady drizzle until all the oil has been added. Mix in the lemon juice, capers, cornichons, baby onions and herbs. Season and set aside.

In a large saucepan, heat half the butter with the oil over a low to medium heat. Cut the bacon into large lardons, add to the pan and cook until crispy. Add the onions, cook for 5 minutes, stirring occasionally, then stir in the sugar and half the molasses. Allow the sugar to dissolve. When it's bubbling, stir in the mustard powder and cook for 5–10 minutes until thick and syrupy. Stir through the remaining molasses, the beans and the parsley.

Put the clams into a pan with a little water. Cover, place over a medium to high heat and bring to the boil. Steam for 1 minute to open the shells. Cool a little and remove the clams from the shells.

Heat the vegetable oil in a deep-fat fryer to 180°C/350°F or in a deep heavy-based saucepan until a breadcrumb sizzles and turns brown when dropped into it. Note: hot oil can be dangerous; do not leave it unattended. Line a large plate with kitchen paper.

Pour the evaporated milk into a bowl and mix the cornmeal and flour in a separate bowl. Season the flour mixture. Dip the clams first in the milk then in the flour mixture and deep-fry for 1–2 minutes. Drain on the kitchen paper and sprinkle with salt.

Slice the buns, two-thirds of the way through. Fill with lettuce, top with the clams and the tartare sauce. Serve with the beans.

We cooked this dish at the House of the Seven Gables after we had had a spell put on us by Lorelei, one of Salem's famous witches. To say it was a surreal experience would be an understatement! This dish is a Salem classic. Usually made on the beach, an old sack soaked in water is placed over the top of the fish, and the moisture from the seaweed cooks everything underneath. We didn't have an old sack so we used a bath towel from the hotel (that won't be going back!).

SALEM SEAFOOD FEAST

SERVES 10

10 tomatillos
2kg (4½ lb) fresh seaweed
2 corn on the cob
2 raw lobsters, each cut
  in half lengthways
1kg (2¼ lb) clams
1kg (2¼ lb) mussels
1 whole crab, cut in half
1kg (2¼ lb) prawns (shrimp)
2 x 150g (5 oz) salmon fillets,
  skinned
300g (10½ oz) swordfish
300g (10½ oz) halibut
1 large baguette
olive oil, to drizzle
2 lemons, cut into wedges

For the butter
500g (2¼ cups) butter,
  at room temperature
1 whole garlic bulb, chopped
1 teaspoon lemon salt or sea salt
1 teaspoon lemon pepper
1 teaspoon pink peppercorns,
  crushed
100g (3½ oz) hazelnuts, chopped
3 tablespoons freshly chopped
  flat-leaf parsley
2 tablespoons dried dulse powder

First, make the butter. Put all the ingredients together in a bowl and mix together with a wooden spoon.

To cook the tomatillos, melt half the butter in a shallow pan. Pull the skins back on the tomatillos then pop them into the butter. Cook gently for 5 minutes, then take the pan off the heat.

To cook the seafood, place a very large roasting tray on a hob over a high heat – you may need to put a couple of rings on to heat the whole tray. Cover the bottom of the tray with the seaweed, then pour over 200ml (1 cup) water. Slice each corn on the cob into five rounds. Arrange the seafood and the corn over the top, then cover with a wet tea towel – or two if yours isn't large enough to cover it – and steam for 20–30 minutes.

Meanwhile, heat a griddle pan until hot. Cut the baguette in half lengthways, drizzle with olive oil and char, cut-side down, on the griddle. Cut the halves in half again if they don't fit into the griddle pan. Smother in butter.

Pour the remaining butter over the seafood, pop the tomatillos into the seafood pot, along with the lemon wedges, and serve with the bread.

We discovered a fascinating art shop in Salem. Following an old Japanese technique, the artist there paints ink onto real fish and prints it onto paper. Fishermen were coming in with tuna tails 2 or 3 feet wide, to be printed and framed for posterity. They looked amazing. I couldn't resist cooking up some of the local catch. Try not to blend the tuna too much – leave it chunky.

TUNA BURGERS
WITH LIME & YUZU MAYO

=== SERVES 4 ===

For the burger
500g (1 lb 2 oz) tuna,
  cut into chunks
1 medium egg white
2cm (¾ in) piece fresh root ginger,
  peeled and grated
2 teaspoons soy sauce
1 lime, juiced
sea salt and freshly ground
  black pepper
small bunch of coriander
  (cilantro)

For the lime and yuzu mayo
2 medium egg yolks
1 teaspoon Dijon mustard
200ml (1 cup) vegetable oil
1 lime, juiced
1 teaspoon yuzu juice

To serve
4 tablespoons vegetable oil
4 burger buns, halved
4 baby cucumbers,
  sliced lengthways
1 butterhead lettuce, quartered
4 large pickled onions, sliced

Put the tuna into a food processor and pulse for 10 seconds. Place in a large bowl and stir in the egg white. Add the ginger, soy sauce and lime juice, then season with black pepper. Chop a third of the coriander (cilantro) and mix in, too.

Divide the mixture into four rough portions then shape each one into a burger-shaped round. Be careful not to compress the mixture too tightly.

For the lime and yuzu mayo, whisk the egg yolks and mustard together in a medium bowl. Slowly pour the vegetable oil into the bowl, a drizzle at a time, whisking well, until the mixture has thickened. Finally, whisk in the lime juice and yuzu juice.

Drizzle 2 tablespoons vegetable oil into a large non-stick frying pan and place over a medium heat. Once the oil is hot, toast the cut side of the buns. Put to one side.

Drizzle the remaining oil into the pan and cook the tuna burgers for 1–2 minutes on each side, then flip over and cook for another minute.

Put a burger base onto a board, then layer up a quarter of the coriander, a halved cucumber and a burger. Put the lettuce on top, then a large dollop of the lime and yuzu mayo. Scatter over the pickled onion slices. Finish by adding the top of the bun to the burger and place on a platter. Assemble the other three burgers in the same way and serve.

WELCOME
TO THE
VILLAGE OF SAG HARBOR

NO WAKE ZONE
5 MPH
DOCKMASTERS ANSWER CH 9

Turbot can be very expensive, but my god it's good when cooked on the bone and served whole. This is the kind of dinner-party dish you might expect to be served in The Hamptons, not that I have ever been invited for dinner there! If I end up working as a chef for a family in The Hamptons one day, this is what I would cook for them and their guests.

TURBOT
WITH PUMPKIN & PEAS

=== SERVES 6 ===

500g (1 lb 2 oz) pumpkin, chopped into large chunks
1 butternut squash, chopped into large chunks
1 fennel bulb, sliced
2 tablespoons butter
sea salt and freshly ground black pepper
1kg (2¼ lb) turbot on the bone
1 lemon, juiced
200g (7 oz) bacon, preferably streaky
4 tablespoons white wine
500ml (2 cups) chicken stock
200ml (1 cup) double (heavy) cream
250g (9 oz) peas

To serve
fennel fronds and bergamot leaves (optional)

Preheat the oven to 240°C/475°F/gas mark 9.

Place the pumpkin, squash and fennel into a roasting tray. Dot with butter, season and place the turbot on top, then pour over the lemon juice and season. Lay the slices of bacon on top of the fish and around the tray.

Pour over the wine and chicken stock. Bake in the oven for 25–30 minutes.

Drain the liquor from the roasting tray into a large saucepan, place over a medium heat and bring to the boil. Pour in the cream, add the remaining butter and season. Add the peas and bring to the boil.

Spoon the sauce, along with the peas, over the vegetables and the fish. Sprinkle with fennel fronds and bergamot leaves (if using).

The earthy flavour of quinoa is unique, and goes brilliantly with monkfish and scallops, which I got from Reading Terminal Market in the heart of Philadelphia. It is an interesting place, but you need to time your visit right – some days they get 100,000 people through the doors.

SCALLOP & MONKFISH
WITH BEURRE NOISETTE, QUINOA & TOMATO SALAD

=== SERVES 4 ===

5 x 5cm (2 in) pieces of
  fresh turmeric
150g (5 oz) red quinoa
sea salt and freshly ground
  black pepper
150g (⅔ cup) salted butter
25g (1 oz) semi-dried
  tomatoes, chopped
1 tablespoon freshly
  chopped dill
1 tablespoon freshly
  chopped mint
1 tablespoon freshly
  chopped basil
1 tablespoon freshly
  chopped chives
1 lemon, juiced
5 key limes or 2 limes, juiced
2 tablespoons olive oil,
  plus extra for drizzling
12 large Atlantic
  hand-dived scallops
4 x 100g (3½ oz) monkfish fillets
400g (14 oz) mixed tomatoes,
  such as beef tomatoes, green,
  San Marzano, cherry
100g (½ cup) cream cheese
  with wood roasted peppers
2 tablespoons balsamic vinegar

To serve
extra herbs (optional)

Place the turmeric in a medium saucepan and pour in 300ml (1¼ cups) water. Cover with a lid and bring to the boil. Pour the quinoa into a bowl and when the turmeric stock has come to the boil, pour over the top, season and leave to soak for 10 minutes.

In the same pan, add 100g (½ cup) of the butter and heat gently. As soon as it's melted, turn up the heat slightly and cook until the liquid is nut brown and foaming. Add the soaked quinoa, the semi-dried tomatoes and all the herbs. Pour over half the lemon juice and all of the lime juice, season and stir everything together then continue to cook for 5 minutes over a medium heat.

Pour the olive oil into a large non-stick frying pan and place over a high heat. As soon as the oil is hot, pop the scallops and monkfish into the pan and cook for 2–3 minutes. Don't be tempted to move the fish around otherwise they won't brown properly – the pieces should be a deep golden colour. Season, then flip over and add the remaining butter to the pan. Once the butter has melted, spoon over the fish and cook for a further 2 minutes. You may need to cook the fish in batches.

Prepare the tomatoes by slicing the large ones and cutting the baby or cherry tomatoes in half.

Spread the cream cheese in a thin layer over a large platter. Arrange the tomatoes over one half of the cream cheese and the quinoa salad over the other. Drizzle the remaining lemon juice over the fish, then spoon all the fish on top of the two salads. Drizzle with the balsamic and olive oil. Garnish with a few extra herbs, if desired.

MEAT

I cooked this in the grounds of Raymond Vineyards in Napa Valley, underneath one of the biggest fig trees I have ever seen. What a place to visit... unlike any other vineyard. I even got the chance to blend my own wine (named after my dog, Ralph). Garlic risotto with steak is a dish I tried when I first visited Napa 20 years ago and I still remember the taste.

GARLIC RISOTTO
WITH MAPLE SALTED STEAK

=== SERVES 4 ===

For the risotto
2 garlic bulbs
1 tablespoon olive oil
sea salt and freshly ground
  black pepper
4 tablespoons butter
2 shallots, diced
100g (3½ oz) arborio rice
1 teaspoon savory leaves,
  chopped (optional)
600ml (2½ cups) hot
  chicken stock
4 tablespoons white wine
25g (1 oz) Parmesan cheese
2 tablespoons freshly
  chopped chives
1 tablespoon chive flowers

For the maple salted steak
2 tablespoons olive oil
2 x 300g (10½ oz) sirloin
  steak, eye only
2 tablespoons butter
1 teaspoon maple salt
  or sea salt

Preheat the oven to 200°C/400°F/gas mark 6.

Cut the tops off the garlic bulbs and place in a small square of foil. Drizzle with the oil, season with salt and pepper, then wrap up into a parcel and secure tightly. Place on a baking sheet and roast in the oven for 30 minutes.

To make the risotto, heat the butter in a medium saucepan over a low heat and fry the shallots gently until softened but not coloured. Stir in the rice and savory (if using) and coat in the buttery shallots.

Pour the stock and wine into the pan and simmer, stirring occasionally, for 20 minutes.

For the maple salted steaks, heat a heavy-based frying pan until hot. Drizzle in the oil then add the steaks. Cook over a medium heat for 2–3 minutes on each side.

Add the butter to the pan and, once melted and foaming, spoon over the steaks. Season with maple salt and pepper, transfer to a board and rest for 5 minutes.

To finish the risotto, squeeze the roasted garlic out of the bulbs and add to the pan. Stir through the risotto then grate over the Parmesan and sprinkle over the chopped chives. Season to taste with salt and pepper and stir everything again.

Spoon the risotto onto plates. Slice the steaks and place on top of the risotto. Sprinkle over the chive flowers and serve.

Chipotle chillies are smoked dried jalapeños, used a lot in the States. They vary in heat, from mild through to very spicy and have a distinct smoky flavour, which goes brilliantly in this butter with steak, but also works really well with beans and lentils in a vegetarian dish.

RIB-EYE STEAK
WITH CHIPOTLE BUTTER, CORN & BIBB SALAD

=== SERVES 4 ===

2 x 500g (1 lb 2 oz) rib-eye steaks
2 tablespoons olive oil
4 large corn on the cob

For the chipotle butter
4 dried chipotle chillies
300g (1⅓ cups) butter, softened
2 tablespoons freshly
  chopped mint
2 tablespoons freshly chopped
  coriander (cilantro)
3 limes, zested and juiced
1 tomato, deseeded and diced
sea salt and freshly ground
  black pepper

For the Bibb salad
1 Bibb lettuce or butter lettuce
2 avocados, peeled and sliced
½ cactus fruit, peeled and
  cut lengthways (optional)
4 plum tomatoes, quartered
1 tablespoon freshly chopped
  coriander (cilantro)
1 tablespoon freshly
  chopped mint

The night before, put the dried chillies for the chipotle butter in a bowl of cold water and leave to soak overnight.

The next day, preheat the barbecue: when the coals are silvery in colour, it's ready.

Make the chipotle butter. Drain the chipotle chillies, trim the stalks and chop finely. Put them in a bowl then add the rest of the ingredients, mix everything together and season with salt and pepper. Put half the butter into a saucepan. Cover the bowl of remaining butter and place in the fridge to chill. Melt the butter in the pan over a low heat.

Rub the steaks with olive oil and season with salt and pepper. Place onto the barbecue and cook for 6 minutes then turn over. Cook for a further 6 minutes. (If you like your steak well done, cook for another minute or so on each side.) Put on a plate to rest.

Pull the husks off the corn. Place the cobs onto the barbecue. Cook for 6 minutes, turning halfway through. Brush the melted butter over the steaks and the corn while cooking, to baste.

Meanwhile, make the Bibb salad. Plunge the whole lettuce into a bowl of iced water – this makes the leaves really crispy. Drain well, then separate the leaves.

Arrange the leaves on a large serving plate and spoon the avocado, cactus fruit and tomatoes on top to fill the leaves. Sprinkle over the herbs.

Slice the steaks on a board and put on a serving plate. Top with a large spoonful of the chilled butter, place the corns alongside and serve with the salad.

No visit to Austin would be complete without a trip to Allens Boots. Everybody (and I mean everybody) wears cowboy boots in this town, even businessmen, with their suits. But if you want to get dressed up as a real Texan, take your credit card with you, as cowboy boots range in price from $15 to $15,000! After a spot of shopping, we visited another Austin institution – Torchy's – to try their meatball tacos.

CHEESY TEXAS MEATBALLS

SERVES 6

For the sauce
2 tablespoons olive oil
1 onion, finely diced
8 garlic cloves, crushed
2 red peppers (bell peppers),
  deseeded and diced
6 tomatoes, quartered
400g (14 oz) tin
  chopped tomatoes
400ml (1¾ cups) filter coffee
4 tablespoons dark brown sugar
2 tablespoons black treacle
100ml (½ cup) tomato ketchup
4 tablespoons red wine
  vinegar or 2 tablespoons
  Worcestershire sauce
1 red chilli, sliced
3 star anise
1 teaspoon dried oregano
2 teaspoons smoked paprika
400g (14 oz) tin kidney
  beans, drained

For the meatballs
1kg (2¼ lb) lean minced
  (ground) beef
2 tablespoons panko
  breadcrumbs
1 medium egg
1 medium egg yolk
1 tablespoon Dijon mustard
sea salt and freshly ground
  black pepper
200g (7 oz) Cheddar
  cheese, finely grated

Heat the oil in a large casserole dish and fry the onion and garlic for a few minutes. Add the peppers and stir in then add the fresh and tinned tomatoes, coffee, brown sugar, treacle, tomato ketchup, vinegar (or Worcestershire sauce), chilli, oregano, spices and kidney beans. Bring to the boil and simmer for 10 minutes.

Put the mince into a large bowl. Add the breadcrumbs, egg and egg yolk and mustard, and season well. Mix everything together thoroughly. Divide the mixture into 12 and shape into balls.

Remove and discard the star anise from the sauce and taste and adjust the seasoning of the sauce. Drop the meatballs in and gently simmer for 5–10 minutes, turning occasionally.

Preheat the grill (broiler).

Once the meatballs are cooked, sprinkle a pile of the grated cheese over each meatball and place under the grill for a couple of minutes until bubbling and golden.

Short ribs are taken from the top of the rib joint and are sometimes known as 'Jacob's ladder'. They need to be cooked for at least a couple of hours to soften, then coated in sauce, before being baked or barbecued. The meat should just fall apart. The idea for this dish came from Black's Barbecue restaurant in Austin.

BEEF RIBS
WITH SUCCOTASH & BOURBON BBQ SAUCE

=== SERVES 4 ===

2kg (4½ lb) beef ribs
1 head of celery, halved
1 onion, halved
2 carrots
small bunch of flat-leaf parsley

For the bourbon BBQ sauce
2 tablespoons olive oil
2 onions, sliced
15cm (6 in) piece fresh root
  ginger, peeled and diced
cloves from 1 garlic bulb, crushed
300g (1½ cups) brown sugar
100ml (½ cup) soy sauce
4 tablespoons red wine vinegar
750ml (3 cups) tomato ketchup
200ml (1 cup) bourbon whiskey

For the succotash (warm salad)
2 tablespoons olive oil
100g (½ cup) butter
the corn cut from 2 corn
  on the cob
300g (2½ cups) broad beans
  (fava beans)
3 chillies, sliced
small bunch of mint, chopped
small bunch of parsley, chopped
sea salt and freshly ground
  black pepper

Put the beef ribs into a large casserole dish. Add the celery, onion, carrots and parsley. Pour enough cold water over the top to cover, then put a lid on the pan and bring to the boil. Reduce the heat and simmer for 3 hours.

Preheat the oven to 220°C/425°F/gas mark 7.

To make the bourbon BBQ sauce, heat the oil in a large saucepan and cook the onions over a medium heat for about 2–3 minutes. Stir in the ginger and garlic, then add the sugar, soy sauce, red wine vinegar, ketchup and bourbon. Bring the mixture to the boil and simmer for a few minutes.

When the beef is ready, lift it out of the liquid and discard the liquid and vegetables, or strain and reserve to use for stock. Put it into a roasting tray, pour the sauce over the top and roast for 20 minutes.

To make the succotash, heat the oil and 4 tablespoons of the butter in a hot pan. Once the butter has melted, add the corn and cook for a few minutes until golden. Add the broad beans (fava beans) to the pan, along with the chillies, mint and parsley, then season. Heat on the hob for a couple of minutes to warm though, then add the rest of the butter and heat to melt.

Spoon the succotash into a bowl and carve the beef into four ribs – one for each person. Coat the beef with the sauce and serve.

Angelo's in Fort Worth was one of the best places I visited. From the outside, it looks like a rundown wooden shack. It would once have stood alone in the middle of a ranch or open field, but is now in the centre of an industrial estate, around which the town has grown. Packed to the rafters with all kinds of customers – from lawyers and sheriffs to school kids, and of course tourists – this was THE place for barbecue meat. Apparently the kitchen gets through over 2,000 pounds of beef per day. My version of beef brisket is easy to make, and not cooked with any spices (although you can add some if you like).

BEEF BRISKET BUNS
WITH SLAW

=== SERVES 4 ===

1.5kg (3 lb) beef brisket
568ml (19 fl oz) bottle of bitter
1 litre (5 cups) beef stock
1 tablespoon olive oil
4 brioche buns, halved
8 little gem lettuce leaves

For the slaw
2 medium egg yolks
2 teaspoons Dijon mustard
1 tablespoon white wine vinegar
200ml (1 cup) vegetable oil
¼ red cabbage, shredded
¼ white cabbage, shredded
sea salt and freshly ground
  black pepper
2 red chillies, diced

Preheat the oven to 140°C/275°F/gas mark 1.

Place the brisket in a large ovenproof saucepan, pour in the bitter and beef stock, cover in foil and put into the oven for 3–4 hours.

To make a mayonnaise for the slaw, whisk the egg yolks, mustard and vinegar together in a large bowl. Slowly pour the vegetable oil into the bowl, a drizzle at a time, whisking well until the mixture has thickened.

Put both types of cabbage in a large bowl, sprinkle over 1 teaspoon salt and leave for 5 minutes.

Drizzle the olive oil into a frying pan. Heat until hot and toast the buns, cut-side down, until golden.

Wash the salt off the cabbage and drain. Add to the bowl of mayonnaise, along with the chillies, and mix together. Season to taste.

To serve, carve the brisket into thin slices. Place the lettuce on the brioche bases, top with the brisket and slaw and serve with the other halves on top.

Making this dish was the best day of filming I've ever had, in the best location. It looked like something from a film set but it was 100% real. There was no sink, no chopping board, with everything balanced on an upturned old bird box, but what a view! It was followed by one of the best sunsets I have ever seen, and then a trip to Billy Bob's, one of the biggest nightclubs in Texas, with live country music, line-dancing, pool tables, an indoor rodeo and real-life armadillo racing! I love America...

BBQ MEAT FEST

=== SERVES 6 ===

4 tablespoons olive oil
500g (1 lb 2 oz) rib-eye steak
3 x 250g (9 oz) pork chops
3 beef sausages
3 pork sausages
sea salt and freshly ground
   black pepper

For the potatoes
600g (1 lb 5 oz) small
   new potatoes
4 tablespoons olive oil
1 garlic bulb
3 rosemary sprigs,
   leaves picked

For the BBQ sauce
250ml (1 cup) tomato ketchup
2 tablespoons champagne
   vinegar or white wine vinegar
1 shallot, diced
1 garlic clove, crushed
4 tablespoons bourbon whiskey
4 tablespoons maple syrup
2 tablespoons molasses
1 eating apple, cored and chopped

Preheat the barbecue: when the coals are silvery in colour, it's ready.

Brush the oil all over the meat and place on the barbecue and season. Cook for 10 minutes turning occasionally until cooked through.

Tear a large square of heavy-duty foil, big enough to hold the potatoes and be wrapped up into a parcel. Drizzle the oil over the top and scatter over the garlic and rosemary. Season well. Wrap up into a parcel, place on to the coals and cook for 8–10 minutes.

Place all the ingredients for the BBQ sauce in a pan and season. Stir everything together and pop onto the barbecue for 5 minutes to heat through.

Arrange all the meat on a large board and season. Slice the steak and halve the chops and sausages. Spoon the sauce over the top and serve with the potatoes.

Pulled pork is a US tradition that has been around for nearly a century –
it's basically on every menu around Fort Worth. Texan portions are huge,
and I came up with this recipe to use up some pork which was left over
from lunch the previous day.

LOADED POTATO SKINS
WITH PULLED PORK & SMOKED BACON

=== SERVES 10 ===

10 large baking potatoes
2 x 300g (10½ oz) pork fillets

For the BBQ sauce
150g (¾ cup) soft brown sugar
2 tablespoons Worcestershire
 sauce
200ml (1 cup) tomato ketchup
sea salt and freshly ground
 black pepper

For the filling
1 tablespoon olive oil
100g (3½ oz) streaky bacon,
 preferably smoked, chopped
 into 1cm (½ in) pieces
the corn cut from 1 corn
 on the cob
5 spring onions (scallions),
 finely chopped
small bunch of flat-leaf
 parsley, chopped
200g (7 oz) Cheddar
 cheese, grated

Preheat the oven to 160°C/325°F/gas mark 3.

Score each potato across the top and bake for 1½ hours.
Cool the potatoes and use a spoon to scoop the flesh into a
bowl. Set the skins aside on a plate. Turn the oven down to
140°C/275°F/gas mark 1.

To make the pulled pork, cut the pork fillets in half and place
in a deep roasting tray. Sprinkle over the brown sugar, then add
the Worcestershire sauce and ketchup. Stir everything together
and season. Cover in foil and braise in the oven for 2 hours.

Make the filling. Heat the oil in a large frying pan and fry
the bacon until crispy. Add the corn to the bacon and cook
for 2–3 minutes until golden, then add the spring onions
(scallions) and parsley. Take the pan off the heat.

Drain the BBQ sauce from cooking the pork into a bowl.
Then use two forks to shred the cooked pork. Add half the
potato flesh to the tray, then the bacon and corn mix. Stir
thoroughly then add the rest of the potato flesh and season.

Preheat the grill (broiler).

Put the potato skins onto a shallow, lipped baking sheet
and stuff the mixture into them so they are overly full. Scatter
the cheese over the top and spoon over some of the remaining
BBQ sauce.

Grill the loaded potato skins for around 5 minutes until
the cheese is melting and bubbling. Serve on a large platter.

The Lobster Tamale Pie I had at the Flora Street Café in Dallas must
be one of the best ways to eat lobster. The dish, created by Stephan Pyles,
has taken the city by storm. This is another of my favourite lobster
dishes – a decadent take on a comfort food classic.

BAKED LOBSTER MAC 'N' CHEESE & TOMAHAWK STEAK

≡ SERVES 6 ≡

For the mac 'n' cheese
1 tablespoon sea salt,
   plus extra for seasoning
500g (1 lb 2 oz) macaroni
2 tablespoons butter
2 tablespoons plain
   (all-purpose) flour
4 tablespoons white wine
300ml (1¼ cups) milk
300ml (1¼ cups) double
   (heavy) cream
2 bay leaves
freshly ground black pepper
2 cooked lobsters,
   meat removed
small bunch of flat-leaf
   parsley, chopped
300g (10½ oz) Cheddar
   cheese, grated

For the steaks
2 x 500g (1 lb 2 oz) Tomahawk
   or rib-eye steaks
1 beef stock cube
olive oil, for drizzling
1 garlic bulb, halved horizontally

Preheat the oven to 240°C/475°F/gas mark 9.

Bring a large pan of water to the boil, add the salt and
the macaroni, bring to the boil and cook over a low-ish heat
for 8–10 minutes (or according to timings on the pack),
stirring occasionally.

Put the steaks on a board. Crumble the stock cube over the
top to season the steaks. Place a large ovenproof frying pan over
a medium heat and, when hot, drizzle in the oil. Add the steaks
to the pan and sear all over then add the garlic and transfer to
the oven for 15 minutes to cook. Take the pan out of the oven,
cover and set aside to rest for 10 minutes.

Drain the pasta, then rinse under cold running water to cool.

In the same pan, melt the butter. Once melted, whisk in the
flour to make a roux. Cook on the hob, stirring the mixture, for
30 seconds. Pour in the white wine and stir in to deglaze the pan,
then whisk in the milk and cream over a low to medium heat.
Add the bay leaves and gently simmer for 3–4 minutes until
the mixture has thickened. Season.

Cut the lobster meat into large chunks, reserving any juices,
and add to the sauce with the juices, the macaroni and chopped
parsley. Taste to check the seasoning.

Preheat the grill (broiler). Spoon the mixture into a large roasting
tray and scatter the cheese over the top. Grill for 5–8 minutes.

Put the steaks onto a platter with the garlic and pan juices.
Slice the steak and serve with the lobster mac 'n' cheese.

This dish is Louisiana through and through, and not to be confused with another Louisiana classic, gumbo. Gumbo includes okra and filé powder, made with ground sassafras leaves, which thickens the mixture. It is usually served over rice whereas the rice in Jambalaya is cooked with all the other ingredients. The most important thing to remember is to include the Louisiana holy trinity of onions, celery and green bell pepper. Don't add the prawns (shrimp) until almost at the very end. Think of this as the Louisiana version of paella.

MEATY JAMBALAYA

=== SERVES 6 ===

4 tablespoons olive oil
2 red onions, diced
3 celery sticks, diced
1 green pepper (bell pepper), deseeded and diced
2 green chillies, diced
5 garlic cloves, chopped
1 teaspoon dried thyme
2 teaspoons dried oregano
1 teaspoon chilli powder
1 tablespoon smoked paprika
1 teaspoon freshly ground white pepper
3 x 200g (7 oz) skinless, boneless chicken breasts, halved
200g (7 oz) chorizo sausage, sliced
200g (7 oz) pulled pork (for recipe, see page 148)
125g (¾ cup) long-grain rice
1 litre (5 cups) chicken stock
4 tomatoes, quartered
500g (1 lb 2 oz) shell-on prawns (shrimp)
2 tablespoons butter
sea salt and freshly ground black pepper

Heat half the oil in a large non-stick casserole dish, stir in the onions, celery and pepper and cook over a low to medium heat for 2 minutes. Add the chilli and garlic and stir in.

Mix all the herbs and spices together in a bowl.

In a large frying pan, heat the remaining oil and fry the chicken breasts for 5–6 minutes until golden on each side, turning halfway through.

Add the chorizo to the vegetables, then stir in 4 heaped teaspoons of the spice mix. Add the chicken and pulled pork to the pan, then stir in the rice, pour over the stock and bring to the boil. Add the tomatoes then simmer with the lid on for 20–25 minutes.

Add the prawns (shrimp) and cook for 3–4 minutes.
Dot the butter over the top, stir in to melt, season and serve.

This is a classic dish that was popular in the 1950s and 1960s, both in the States and in Australia. Made with oysters from the Jolie Pearl Oyster Bar in Baton Rouge, it tasted great. The chef there is not a fancy Michelin-starred chef, just a really great cook who loves his food.

CARPET BAGGER'S STEAK
WITH SAUTEED POTATOES & CREAMED SPINACH

===== SERVES 4 =====

10 fresh oysters in shells
  (or from a jar if you can't
  find fresh)
pinch of cayenne pepper
600g (1 lb 5 oz) fillet steak,
  cut from the centre of
  the fillet
sea salt and freshly ground
  black pepper
4 tablespoons butter,
  plus a little extra
1 tablespoon olive oil
100g (3½ oz) streaky bacon,
  cut into lardons
600g (1 lb 5 oz) new potatoes,
  cooked for 10 minutes,
  quartered
100g (3½ oz) baby leaf
  spinach, washed
4 tablespoons double
  (heavy) cream

Preheat the oven to 220°C/425°F/gas mark 7.

Open the oysters by holding each one in a tea towel, rounded side down, with the hinge towards you. Using an oyster or butter knife, wiggle it in and use a firm hand to loosen the hinge, then run the knife all around the rim to lift off the lid. Put the oysters and the juice into a bowl. Season with the pinch of cayenne.

Cut the beef in half and make a pocket in the middle of each, about 2cm (1 in) from the edge. Stuff the oysters into each pocket. Tie each piece of beef with string to hold the oysters in, both vertically and horizontally so the oysters are secure inside. Season.

Heat a large non-stick frying pan over a medium heat until hot and add the butter. Once the butter has melted, add the steak to the pan and fry all over to seal. Lift into a roasting tray and roast for 15–20 minutes.

Cook the potatoes. Drizzle the oil into an ovenproof pan and heat over a medium heat. Add the bacon and cook until golden and crisp then add the potatoes, a knob of butter and season well. Toss everything together and place in the oven for 8–10 minutes.

Take the beef out of the oven, baste in the juices, cover and set aside to rest.

For the creamed spinach, melt a knob of butter in a saucepan, over a medium heat. When the butter is foaming, add the spinach, season and pour in the cream. Bring to the boil, toss to coat the spinach in the sauce and cook for 1 minute.

To serve, snip the string off the beef and carve each piece into two smaller steaks. Serve with the spinach and potatoes.

About eight hours before the Louisiana State University football game, 4,000 pick-up trucks, often with in-built TVs and barbecues, arrived in the stadium car park and dropped their tailgates. People cooked all manner of things on their barbecues, from ribs to alligator and even raccoon... I got this recipe from a gentleman called Clive, who was making it on his barbecue alongside some armadillo steaks!

PORK RIBS
WITH APPLE & FENNEL

=== SERVES 4–6 ===

For the ribs
1.5kg (3 lb) pork ribs
3 leeks, halved
2 shallots, halved
2 x 5cm (2 in) pieces
  fresh root ginger,
  peeled and chopped
1 tablespoon fennel seeds
750ml (3¼ cups) apple juice

For the BBQ sauce
300g (1½ cups) dark
  brown sugar
750ml (3¼ cups) tomato ketchup
100ml (½ cup) soy sauce
4 tablespoons white
  wine vinegar
1 teaspoon fennel seeds
3 garlic cloves, crushed
4 Cox's apples, grated
5cm (2 in) piece fresh root
  ginger, peeled and diced
3 oranges, juiced
1 tablespoon smoked paprika

Put the ribs into a large pan. Add the leeks, shallots, ginger and fennel seeds, then pour in the apple juice and 750ml (3¼ cups) water to cover. Put a lid on the pan and bring to the boil then simmer for 1½ –2 hours, still covered.

When the ribs have nearly finished simmering, preheat the oven to 230°C/450°F/gas mark 8, then make the BBQ sauce. Place the sugar into a large frying pan, then add the ketchup, soy sauce and vinegar. Heat gently, stirring all the ingredients together, then add the fennel seeds, garlic, grated apple, ginger, orange juice and smoked paprika. Season well and continue to stir everything together until the mixture comes to a simmer, then cook for 2 minutes.

Place the ribs into a roasting tray, pour the sauce over the top and toss to coat the ribs. Place the orange skins in the roasting tray, too, and roast for 20 minutes.

Transfer the ribs and roasted oranges to a large warm platter to serve, spooning the remaining sauce from the tray over the top.

I sampled this dish on a rare day off around Boston. I'd just been handed the keys to a Corvette and I couldn't resist taking it for a spin. Two hundred miles later I headed back into Boston, looking for a meal. I parked up, and 20 minutes later this plate was in front of me: steak with waffles, made with truffle butter. My recipe is slightly different, as the butter made the waffle too soft for me. Think of it as the US take on our ham, egg and chips. It was almost as good as the trip out in the motor.

T-BONE STEAK
& POTATO WAFFLES

=== SERVES 2 ===

For the steak and eggs
sea salt and freshly ground
  black pepper
1 T-bone steak, approx.
  750g (1 lb 10 oz)
1 tablespoon olive oil
4 large spring onions
  (scallions), halved
  lengthways
2 medium eggs

For the potato waffles
250g (2 cups) plain
  (all-purpose) flour
1 tablespoon baking powder
1 teaspoon salt
3 medium eggs
100g (½ cup) butter, softened
75g (2½ oz) potatoes,
  cooked and riced
1 large spring onion
  (scallion), diced
25g (1 oz) Taleggio
  cheese, chopped
1 tablespoon freshly
  chopped tarragon
200ml (1 cup) milk

To serve
1 x 3cm (1¼ in) fresh black
  truffle (optional)

You will also need
  a waffle machine

Preheat the oven to 220°C/425°F/gas mark 7. Heat the waffle machine.

Heat a large non-stick frying pan over a medium heat. Season the steak, drizzle over the oil and fry on one side for 2 minutes. Turn the steak over, then add the halved spring onions (scallions) and place in the oven for 4 minutes.

For the potato waffles, put the flour into a large bowl and add the baking powder, salt, eggs, butter, potato, diced spring onion, cheese, tarragon and milk. Whisk all the ingredients together and season with black pepper.

Ladle the waffle mix into the waffle machine and cook, in batches, for a couple of minutes until golden.

Put the steak onto a warm plate, cover and leave to rest. Put the pan on the hob over a low to medium heat, and fry the spring onions for another couple of minutes. Push the spring onions to one side, then crack the eggs into the pan and fry them in the oil and meat juices for the maximum flavour.

To serve, place the steak on a large platter and spoon the spring onions on the side. Place the waffles on the platter, followed by the eggs. Shave the truffle generously over the top (if using).

I made this dish using the wood-fired oven at the stunning Amber Waves Farm. The Hamptons was a beautiful place, one of my favourites on the trip, but the one thing that will stick in my mind more than anything was the $170 I paid for 12 lamb chops!

LAMB WITH SQUASH, AUBERGINE & TAHINI DRESSING

=== SERVES 8 ===

2 racks of lamb, 8 chops
 on each
2 tablespoons olive oil
salt and freshly ground
 black pepper
1 garlic bulb

For the vegetables
3 small squash or pumpkins,
 1.2kg (2½ lb)
3 green peppers (bell peppers)
4 small aubergines (eggplants)
2 garlic bulbs
4 tablespoons olive oil

For the tahini dressing
5 tablespoons tahini
300g (1½ cups) cream cheese

To serve
2 tablespoons sesame
 seeds, toasted
small bunch of dill, chopped
small bunch of coriander
 (cilantro), chopped
small bunch of mint, chopped
2 red chillies, deseeded and
 finely chopped
1 lime, juiced

Slice the racks of lamb into chops on a board then set aside.

Prepare the vegetables. Cut the squash in half and remove all the seeds then cut into four or five wedges, each around 2cm (¾ in) thick. Halve the peppers and remove the core, then cut each half into two.

Cut the aubergines (eggplants) into quarters lengthways, then halve the garlic bulbs and pop all the vegetables into a large roasting tray. Drizzle over the oil, season well and toss everything together. Pop into the pizza oven for 10 minutes or into a regular oven, preheated to the highest temperature and roast for 20–25 minutes until golden and tender.

Make the tahini dressing. Put the ingredients into a medium bowl, season and fold together.

For the lamb, heat a large roasting tray on the hob over a medium heat until hot – you may need to use two rings if the tray is very large. Drizzle the oil into the tray, then place the chops onto the tray. Season and cook for 2–3 minutes. Flip each one over then cook for a further 2–3 minutes. Take the tray off the heat and rest the chops for a few minutes.

To serve, spread the tahini dressing all over a platter, top with the roasted vegetables and lamb chops, then sprinkle over the sesame seeds, herbs and chillies. Lastly, pour the lime juice over the top and serve.

This was a great dish to fill me up before my monster tour around Philadelphia, with tour guide Owen. You won't see me running on camera very often, but when I found myself at the bottom of the 'Rocky Steps' of the Philadelphia Museum of Art, it had to be done.

PORK TWO WAYS
WITH CARAMELIZED APPLES & BLUE CHEESE

=== SERVES 4 ===

2 tablespoons olive oil
4 x 250g (9 oz) T-bone
 pork chops
4 pork and apple sausages
sea salt and freshly ground
 black pepper
2 eating apples
2 tablespoons salted butter
4 tablespoons dark brown sugar
½ teaspoon ground cinnamon
2 pomegranates
100g (3½ oz) Italian uncut bread
100g (3½ oz) dandelion leaves
 or rocket (arugula)
100g (3½ oz) blue cheese

For the dressing
2 tablespoons pomegranate
 molasses
2 tablespoons white
 wine vinegar
2 tablespoons olive oil
2 black garlic bulbs, chopped

Preheat the oven to the highest temperature.

Heat a large flat, ovenproof griddle pan until hot, drizzle in half the olive oil and pop the pork chops and sausages onto it. Cook for 3–4 minutes, without moving the meat around. Season the meat, then flip each piece over and cook in the oven for 10 minutes.

Cut each apple in half, then cut each half into four wedges. In a non-stick frying pan, melt the butter over a medium heat and sprinkle over the sugar and cinnamon. Add a splash of water – about 1 tablespoon – stir everything together and heat until the sugar has dissolved. When it is bubbling, add the apple and cook gently for 5 minutes. If the sauce thickens, add a splash of water.

Make the dressing. Put the pomegranate molasses, vinegar, oil and garlic in a bowl. Season and whisk together.

Remove the seeds from the pomegranates. Cut each one in half round the equator and place cut-side down in a bowl. Bang the outside with a wooden spoon to extract the seeds.

Take the griddle pan out of the oven and place back on the hob over a medium heat. Tear the bread into large pieces and drop into the pan. Fry in the pork fat, until crisp and like croutons.

Add the dandelion leaves or rocket (arugula) to the same pan and cook for about 1 minute until they've wilted. Crumble over the cheese, then spoon over the apples. Drizzle over the dressing, scatter over the pomegranate seeds and serve.

JAMES' TIP
The flavour of black garlic is not as strong as white garlic, so you will need to use quite a lot.

I made this dish at the end of our journey, standing on Pier A. Right at the bottom of Manhattan Island, I was surrounded by British tourists watching the sunset with the Statue of Liberty in the distance. Cooking a steak with a cold beer in my hand and watching the sun disappear over the horizon was the perfect end to the perfect trip.

NYC STEAK
WITH SPINACH & SALSA VERDE

=== SERVES 4 ===

2 x 500g (1 lb 2 oz) sirloin steaks
sea salt and freshly ground
  black pepper
2 tablespoons olive oil
3 shallots, halved
25g (1 oz) lightly toasted croutons

For the salsa verde
small bunch of basil, chopped
small bunch of flat-leaf
  parsley, chopped
1 shallot, diced
8 anchovy fillets, chopped
3 tablespoons capers, chopped
2 teaspoons Dijon mustard
1 lemon, juiced
100g (3½ oz) candied walnuts
  or walnut halves, chopped
8 tablespoons olive oil

For the spinach
200g (7 oz) baby leaf
  spinach, washed
6 tablespoons double
  (heavy) cream
pinch of freshly
  ground nutmeg

Lay the steaks on a board and season well on both sides. Heat a large non-stick frying pan over a medium heat until hot then drizzle in the oil. Add the steaks and cook for 4–5 minutes then turn each steak over. Add the shallots to the pan, cut-side down, and continue to cook for a further 4–5 minutes. Lift the steaks and shallots onto a warm plate. Cover and leave to rest. Set the pan aside.

Put all the ingredients for the salsa verde into a medium bowl and season well. Mix together.

Place the spinach into the steak frying pan and pour over the cream. Heat over a medium heat for about 1 minute until the spinach has wilted, then season and sprinkle over the nutmeg. Stir everything together.

Slice the steaks on a board. Spoon the spinach over a large platter, arrange the strips of steak on top, spoon over the salsa verde and scatter over the croutons.

In New York, I ate at one of the greatest fish restaurants in the world: Éric Ripert's La Bernadin, a place that I urge you to visit. I had two amazing dishes cooked in front of me, an experience I will never forget. Twenty-four hours later, I felt like eating something completely different. And after all, I had to include a recipe for my version of a classic New York cheeseburger, with a Welsh rarebit topping. Don't buy a burger from a NY street vendor – wait until you get home and cook this one instead.

NYC CHEESEBURGER & FRIES

SERVES 6

For the rarebit
500g (4½ cups) grated
   Cheddar cheese
100ml (3½ fl oz) bitter
1 teaspoon Worcestershire sauce
1 teaspoon Dijon mustard
a few drops of Tabasco
sea salt and freshly ground
   black pepper
4 tablespoons plain
   (all-purpose) flour
1 medium egg yolk

For the burgers
500g (1 lb 2 oz) minced
   (ground) beef
2 tablespoons rapeseed oil

For the fries
1 litre (5 cups) vegetable oil
300g (10½ oz) frozen skinny fries
25g (1 oz) Parmesan cheese

To serve
6 brioche buns, halved
butterhead lettuce
1 red onion, sliced
2 tomatoes, sliced
2 gherkins, sliced

Make the rarebit. Line a 30 x 20cm (12 x 8 in) baking tray with clingfilm (plastic wrap). Place the grated cheese in a medium saucepan, pour in the beer then add the Worcestershire sauce, mustard and Tabasco. Cook over a medium heat, stirring all the time, until the cheese melts.

Season well then stir in the flour and keep stirring until the mixture thickens. Stir in the egg yolk then pour into the lined baking tray and put to one side to set.

Make the burgers. Put the meat into a bowl, season well, mix together and shape into 6 rounds. Rub a little oil over the sides of each burger. Heat a griddle pan. Fry for 2 minutes on each side.

Preheat the grill (broiler). Cut the set rarebit into 6 squares. Place the burgers on a baking tray and top with a square of cheese. Place under the grill for 2 minutes.

Meanwhile, fry the chips. Heat the vegetable oil in a deep-fat fryer to 180°C/350°F or in a deep heavy-based saucepan until a breadcrumb sizzles and turns brown when dropped into it. Note: hot oil can be dangerous; do not leave it unattended. Fry the chips for 4 minutes, drain on kitchen paper and season with salt then transfer them to a plate, grate Parmesan over the top and serve with the burgers.

Toast the brioche buns. Layer up the lettuce, red onions and tomatoes. Top with a burger, gherkins and lid, then repeat until you've assembled all the burgers.

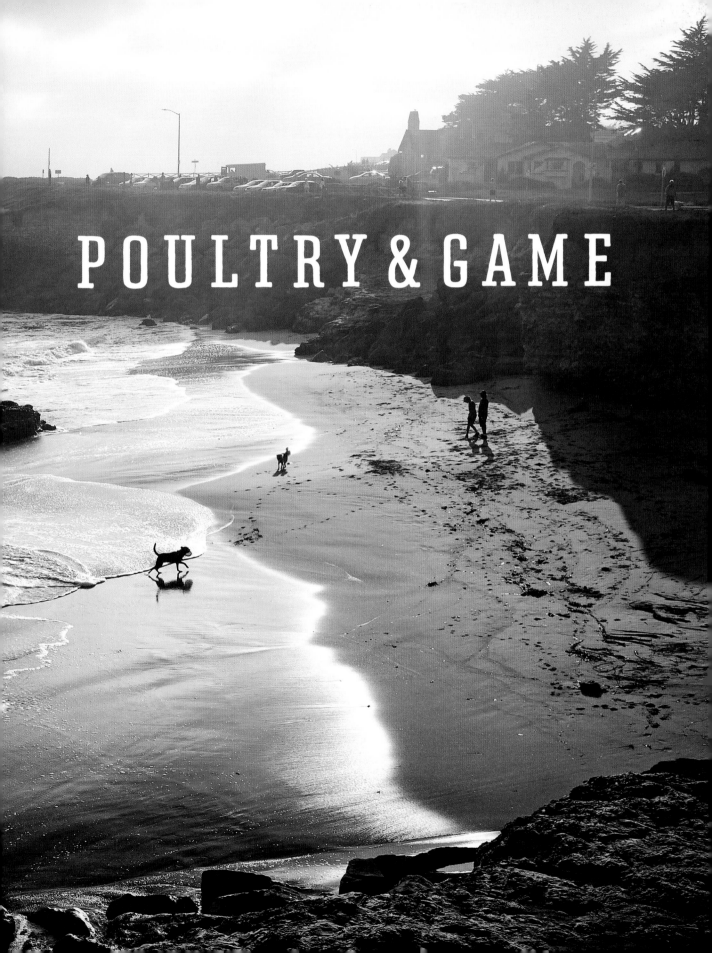

POULTRY & GAME

This dish uses two ingredients that we picked up on the Santa Cruz leg of the trip. We saw strawberries growing all along the coastal roads. The sea air protects them from frost and gives them a unique taste. The honey was bought from a company with a 14-year-old CEO – only in America!

ROASTED DUCK WITH CAVOLO NERO
& STRAWBERRY & PORT SAUCE

=== SERVES 4 ===

4 large duck breasts,
  about 200g (7 oz) each
sea salt and freshly ground
  black pepper
4 tablespoons runny honey
100ml (3½ fl oz) port
400ml (1¾ cups) hot beef stock
100g (3½ oz) kale
100g (3½ oz) cavolo nero
2 tablespoons butter
100g (3½ oz) strawberries,
  halved
30g (1 oz) honeycomb

Preheat the oven to 220°C/425°F/gas mark 7.

Put a large frying pan over a medium heat. Place the duck breasts on a board and remove the fillet from each one and set aside. Season the breasts, lay them in the pan, skin-side down, and cook gently for around 2 minutes to render down the fat.

Turn the duck over, drizzle over the honey and cook for 1 minute. Transfer to an ovenproof dish and roast in the oven for 6–8 minutes, adding the fillets to the dish halfway through.

Put the frying pan back on the hob and pour in the port. Bring to a bubble over a medium heat, then pour in the beef stock. Increase the heat a little and bring to the boil then simmer for around 5 minutes until the sauce has reduced by two-thirds.

Remove the woody stalks from the kale and cavolo nero by cutting either side of each piece and chopping off.

Add a knob of the butter to a sauté pan and place over a medium heat. Add 2 tablespoons of water and once the butter has melted, swirl the pan around to make an emulsion. Add the kale and cavolo nero, season well and cook for 2–3 minutes, tossing every now and then.

Add the remaining butter to the sauce and stir in, then take the pan off the heat and add the strawberries, tossing them through the warm sauce. Take the duck out of the oven, cover and leave to rest for a few minutes.

To serve, spoon the kale and cavolo nero onto a serving platter. Carve each duck breast into slices and place on top. Spoon over the sauce and finish by scattering over the pieces of honeycomb.

One of the highlights of our trip was visiting the Japanese-inspired Single Thread in Sonoma, owned by husband-and-wife team Kyle and Katina Connaughton. Kyle is the head chef, while Katina is in charge of the 15-acre garden. Just three months after opening, the restaurant was awarded two Michelin stars. It is quite possibly the most exciting restaurant you will ever go to in America. The only thing that this dish has in common with the restaurant is the Japanese beer I used. Chopped salad is a staple throughout the US, and is a great accompaniment.

BEER BUTT CHICKEN
WITH CHOPPED SALAD

=== SERVES 4 ===

For the chicken
4 tablespoons smoked paprika
2 tablespoons coriander seeds
2 tablespoons chilli powder
1 lemon, juiced
4 tablespoons olive oil
sea salt and freshly ground
   black pepper
1 large chicken
568ml (20 fl oz) can
   Japanese lager

For the chopped salad
2 heads of chicory, chopped
2 heads of romaine, chopped
½ each yellow, green and
   red pepper (bell pepper)
   deseeded and chopped
½ cucumber, diced
5 spring onions (scallions),
   trimmed and sliced
200g (7 oz) cherry tomatoes
100g (3½ oz) radish
1 corn on the cob,
   kernels removed
small bunch of coriander
   (cilantro), leaves chopped

For the dressing
1 teaspoon Dijon mustard
4 tablespoons white
   wine vinegar
4 tablespoons olive oil

Place the paprika into a large zip-lock bag, big enough to hold the chicken, add the coriander seeds, chilli powder, lemon juice and oil and season well. Open up the cavity of the chicken then place the bird into the bag. Roll the seasoning all over the chicken to coat it. Set aside to marinate.

To make the chopped salad, slice each of the cherry tomatoes in half and put in a large bowl with all the other prepared vegetables, except the coriander (cilantro). Set aside.

Make the dressing. Put the mustard into a small bowl and add the vinegar, oil and 1 tablespoon of water. Season and whisk everything together. Set aside.

Push the opened beer can into the chicken cavity and place on the barbecue. Cover the barbecue with a lid and cook for 30 minutes.

Once the chicken is cooked, lift it onto a board and let it rest for 5 minutes.

Pour the dressing over the chopped salad, add the coriander leaves and season well. Toss everything together.

To serve, lift up the chicken, still sitting on the can, onto a platter and pile the salad around the base.

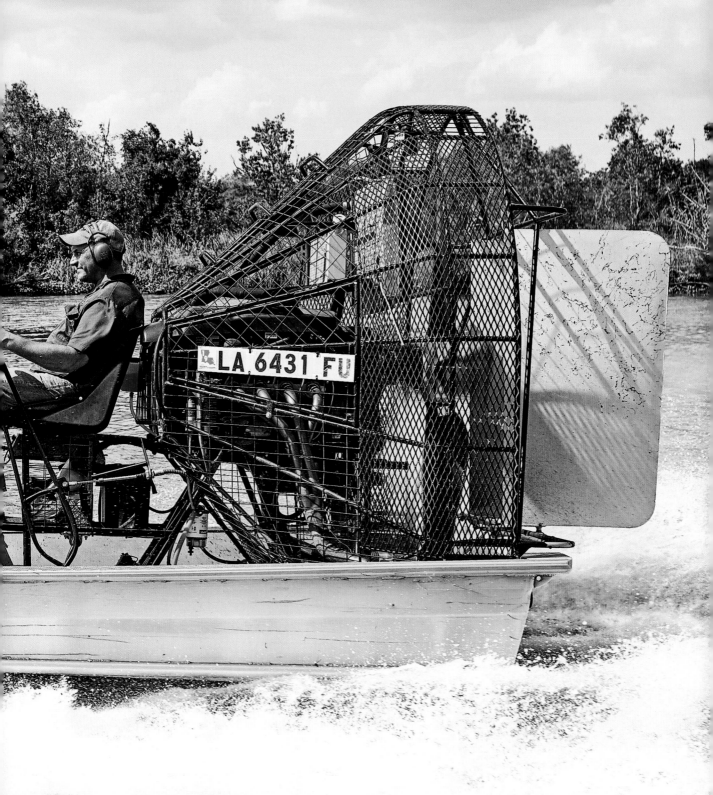

To make this dish I stood in front of the 'You're My Butter Half' mural,
one of many that adorn the streets of Austin. This one is so popular,
the grass in front has worn away – too many people taking selfies!

DEEP-FRIED CHICKEN
& BBQ VEGETABLES

=== SERVES 2 ===

6 heritage carrots
4 small beetroot (beets)
1 litre (35 fl oz) apple juice
100g (¾ cup) plain
  (all-purpose) flour
sea salt and freshly ground
  black pepper
2 medium eggs, beaten
200g (7 oz) yellow corn grits
  or polenta
1 tablespoon BBQ spice rub
500g (2 cups) salted butter
2 x 200g (7 oz) skinless
  chicken breasts
bunch of spring onions
  (scallions), trimmed

For the dressing
2 tablespoons maple syrup
2 tablespoons sherry vinegar
4 tablespoons olive oil
small bunch of tarragon,
  leaves picked and chopped

Preheat the barbecue: when the coals are silvery in colour,
it's ready.

Place the carrots and beetroot (beets) in a large pan and
pour over the apple juice. Cover with a lid and bring to the boil.
Simmer until the vegetables are just cooked, around 10–12 minutes,
then drain well.

Put the flour onto a large plate and season well. Put the eggs
into a separate medium bowl, then mix the yellow corn grits
and BBQ spice rub in a separate large bowl.

Put the butter into a large pan and allow to melt over a medium
heat. Coat each piece of chicken first in the seasoned flour, then
in the beaten egg, then in the spiced grits mixture.

Once the butter is bubbling, lower the chicken breasts into
the pan and cook for 10 minutes, turning halfway through.

Put all the ingredients for the dressing into a medium bowl,
season well and mix together. Spoon a little of the hot butter
from the chicken pan in and whisk in too, for a richer flavour.

Pop the carrots, beetroot and spring onions (scallions) onto
the barbecue. Brush generously with the dressing, and cook
until charred, turning over and brushing more dressing over
as necessary.

Lift the chicken out of the pan, drain on kitchen paper if
necessary, then sprinkle with salt. Put on a board and slice
each piece diagonally into four thick pieces.

To serve, slice the beetroot in half and arrange on a platter,
along with the carrots and spring onions. Top with the chicken
and pour over the remaining dressing.

Bonne femme translates as 'good woman' or 'good wife', and refers to the simplicity of this tasty dish. In culinary terms, it has come to refer to a dish with a mushroom-based sauce. There are lots of versions of Bonne Femme, made using oysters or sole as well as chicken. This is my version of a Louisiana Creole classic. The Worcestershire sauce adds a great depth of flavour.

CHICKEN 'BONNE FEMME'

SERVES 4

4 tablespoons olive oil
100g (3½ oz) lardons or chopped streaky bacon
100g (¾ cup) plain (all-purpose) flour
sea salt and freshly ground black pepper
1.5kg (3 lb) whole chicken, cut into 8 pieces
1 green pepper (bell pepper), deseeded and diced
3 large Spanish onions, sliced
2 celery sticks, diced
125g (4½ oz) white button mushrooms, sliced
300g (10½ oz) new potatoes
5 garlic cloves, chopped
150g (5¼ oz) chorizo sausage, diced
4 tablespoons white wine
2 tablespoons Worcestershire sauce
15 drops of Tabasco
a few sprigs of tarragon

Preheat the oven to 200°C/400°F/gas mark 6.

Place a large roasting tray over a medium heat. Drizzle half the oil into the tray, then add the lardons or bacon. Stir into the hot oil and fry until crispy, tossing every now and then. Once the bacon is cooked, lift out with a slotted spoon and place in a large bowl.

Spread the flour onto a plate and season well. Dip each piece of chicken into it to coat completely. Fry the pieces in the tray, in batches and over a medium heat, adding the remaining oil, as you need to. When each piece is golden on one side, flip over and brown the other side, then place in the bowl with the bacon.

With the tray still over a medium heat, add the vegetables, potatoes, garlic and chorizo, stir in, then pour in the wine. Deglaze, stirring in the sticky bits and juices from the base of the pan, then add the Worcestershire sauce and Tabasco. Return the cooked bacon and chicken to the tray and season.

Transfer to the preheated oven and cook for 35–40 minutes. Sprinkle with tarragon before serving.

This dish was made on Avery Island, in the middle of swamp country. The island is famous for its Tabasco, produced there by the same family business for the last 120 years.

CHIPOTLE BEER CHICKEN
WITH BACON & PECAN COLLARDS

⟹ SERVES 4-6 ⟹

4 skinless, boneless
   chicken breasts
4 skinless, boneless
   chicken thighs
100ml (½ cup) chipotle
   Tabasco sauce
sea salt and freshly ground
   black pepper
4 tablespoons olive oil
300ml (10 fl oz) ale
200g (7 oz) bacon lardons
1 medium onion, diced
2 garlic cloves, crushed
2 tablespoons dark brown sugar
2 tablespoons cider vinegar
4 tablespoons bourbon whiskey
400g (14 oz) tin pinto beans,
   drained
300g (10½ oz) collard greens
   or spring cabbage
4 medium eggs
100g (3½ oz) pecans, chopped

Cut the chicken into large chunks, each around 6 x 3cm (2½ x 1¼ in), then put into a bowl with the chipotle sauce. Season well and mix everything together so that the chicken is well coated.

Heat half the oil in a large non-stick frying pan over a medium heat until hot. Fry the chicken on one side for 2–3 minutes until golden and charred, then flip over the pieces. Do this in two batches if not all the chicken will fit into the pan in one go. Put all the chicken back into the pan if you've done it in batches, then pour in 200ml (1 cup) ale and simmer for 8–10 minutes.

In a separate frying pan, heat the remaining oil over a medium heat and cook the lardons until crispy. Stir in the diced onion and garlic and cook for a further 2–3 minutes. Sprinkle over the sugar, and pour in the vinegar and bourbon. Flambé to burn off the alcohol. Add the pinto beans and warm through, about 2–3 minutes.

Cut the collard greens into large pieces, then roll them up and cut into 2cm (1¾ in) strips. Add half to the bacon mixture and pour over the remaining beer. Simmer over a medium heat to cook the greens down, then add the remaining collards and cook for 1–2 minutes. Strain the juices and sauce from the chicken pan over the greens and stir in.

Season, then make four dips with the back of a spoon in the collard mixture, spaced a little apart. Crack the eggs into the holes. Cover the pan and cook for a couple of minutes until the eggs are cooked. Top with the chicken and pecans and serve.

Most tailgaters fire up the barbecue for ribs and burgers before a football game, so I did something a little different. A classic butter curry – thanks to my mate Vivek Singh. I made enough to feed 60... this recipe is for six.

CHICKEN, SHRIMP & OKRA BUTTER CURRY

⟹ SERVES 6 ⟸

600g (1 lb 5 oz) each skinless, boneless chicken breast
600g (1 lb 5 oz) raw prawns (shrimp), peeled and de-veined

For the marinade
100g (½ cup) Greek yoghurt
2 tablespoons ginger purée
2 tablespoons garlic purée
1 tablespoon vegetable oil
1 tablespoon chilli powder
1 teaspoon ground cumin
½ teaspoon curry powder

For the sauce
4 tablespoons vegetable oil
1 tablespoon ginger purée
1 tablespoon garlic purée
1 teaspoon ground cardamom
1 tablespoon chilli powder
2 teaspoons ground fenugreek
1 teaspoon medium curry powder
2 bay leaves
1 green and 1 red chilli, sliced
4 tomatoes on the vine, halved
sea salt and freshly ground black pepper
2 x 400g (14 oz) tins chopped tomatoes
1 tablespoon caster (superfine) sugar
200g (7 oz) okra
100g (½ cup) salted butter

To garnish
small bunch of coriander (cilantro), leaves chopped
50g (1¾ oz) coconut, shredded
100g (½ cup) Greek yoghurt

Up to eight hours before, marinate the chicken and prawns (shrimp). Cut the chicken into 5 x 2cm (2 x ¾ in) strips. Place all the marinade ingredients into a large bowl and mix together with 1 teaspoon salt. Spoon half into a separate large bowl, then put the chicken in one bowl and the prawns in the other. Stir each well so the prawns and meat are coated completely. Cover and chill.

Preheat the barbecue: when the coals are silvery in colour, it's ready. While the barbecue is heating up, make the sauce. Heat a large non-stick saucepan over a medium heat until hot. Pour in the oil, then add the ginger and garlic purées, the spices, the bay leaves, sliced chillies and fresh tomatoes. Lower the heat slightly, stir everything together and cook for 3–4 minutes.

Season well, then pour in the chopped tomatoes and sugar. Stir everything together and cover the pan with a lid. Simmer very gently over a low heat for 20 minutes.

Meanwhile, lay the pieces of marinated chicken on the barbecue and cook until charred, turning over halfway through. Do the same with the prawns. Lower the charred chicken pieces into the sauce, along with the prawns. Top and tail the okra, then cut each one in half lengthways. Add the okra to the sauce, stir through, cover, then cook for a further 20 minutes.

Cube the butter, add to the pan and stir through the sauce until melted. To serve, sprinkle over the coriander (cilantro) and coconut and dollop on the yoghurt.

Deep-frying is a way of life in the US – in Texas hardware stores, we saw pots and stoves designed specifically for frying a whole chicken. Some were even large enough to deep-fry a whole turkey!

DEEP-FRIED DALLAS CHICKEN
WITH RANCH SALAD

≡ SERVES 4 ≡

4 tablespoons butter
2 tablespoons freshly
  chopped flat-leaf parsley
3 garlic cloves, chopped
sea salt and freshly ground
  black pepper
1.5kg (3¼ lb) whole chicken,
  spatchcocked and wishbone
  removed (see page 210)
vegetable oil, for deep-frying
5 eggs, beaten
2 romaine lettuce, chopped

For the coating
300g (2¼ cups) plain
  (all-purpose) flour
1 tablespoon dried oregano
2 tablespoons smoked paprika
1 tablespoon garlic salt
1 tablespoon celery salt
1 tablespoon dried thyme
1 tablespoon English
  mustard powder

For the ranch dressing
200ml (1 cup) buttermilk
1 teaspoon English
  mustard powder
small bunch of tarragon, chopped
small bunch of coriander
  (cilantro), chopped
small bunch of flat-leaf parsley,
  chopped

For the croutons
4 tablespoons olive oil
3 garlic cloves, sliced
200g (7 oz) unsliced bread,
  torn into small pieces,
  the size of croutons

Line a large plate or baking tray with kitchen paper.

Mix the butter, parsley and garlic together in a bowl and season. Put the chicken on a board and carefully push your fingers under the skin at the neck end to separate it from the flesh. Push the butter in between the skin and the flesh then smooth out evenly.

In a very large pan, pour in enough oil to come halfway up the sides. The oil should cover the chicken when it's submerged. Heat the oil until a breadcrumb sizzles and turns brown when dropped into it. Note: hot oil can be dangerous; do not leave it unattended.

Pop the eggs into a large bowl, big enough to hold the chicken. In a separate, large shallow bowl (again big enough to hold the chicken), mix all the dry ingredients together for the coating and season well. Dip the whole chicken first in the beaten egg then into the coating mixture and repeat.

Once the oil is hot enough, carefully lower the coated chicken into it and deep-fry for 20 minutes until golden and cooked through. To check it's cooked, insert a meat thermometer and test the core temperature – it should be 75°C/170°F or above. Carefully lift the chicken out of the pan, allowing any oil to drain back into it, then set the chicken down on the prepared kitchen paper to drain. Sprinkle with a little salt.

Mix together all the ingredients for the dressing and season.

Make the croutons. Heat the oil in a non-stick frying pan and fry the garlic and bread until golden and crisp. Drain on kitchen paper and sprinkle with a little salt.

To serve, pile the romaine lettuce onto a large platter then scatter over the croutons. Top with the deep-fried chicken and drizzle over the ranch dressing.

SALADS & PASTA

The first time I had this dish cooked for me, it was by the late, great Antonio Carluccio. It's testament to Antonio as a great cook that this was the dish that sprang to mind when I found myself in the middle of a field of artichokes – simple Italian flavours done well. You can use any type of pasta for this. Have a go at preparing fresh artichokes if you haven't done so before – they taste so good.

PASTA WITH ARTICHOKES, CAVOLO NERO & PARMESAN

=== SERVES 4–6 ===

4 tablespoons olive oil
3 garlic cloves, crushed
1 Meyer lemon or an unwaxed lemon, juiced
8 small artichokes
1 tablespoon sea salt
500g (1 lb 2 oz) fresh ziti pasta or dried penne pasta
225g (1 cup) butter, chopped
100g (3½ oz) fresh peas
100g (3½ oz) cavolo nero, shredded
small handful of basil leaves
sea salt and freshly ground black pepper
50g (1¾ cup) Parmesan cheese

Pour the olive oil into a large bowl and stir in the garlic and lemon juice.

Prepare the artichokes by cutting the top off each one, about halfway through the middle, then trim the stalk at the base. Take off all the leaves and use a spoon to scrape out the choke. Discard the leaves and the hairy choke. Use a vegetable peeler to strip away the tough outer peel of each artichoke heart. Cut each into quarters lengthways and add to the olive oil mixture. Stir together.

Bring a large pan of water to the boil, and stir in the salt and pasta. Stir the pasta through the water to loosen the pieces. Cook for 2 minutes, then drain into a bowl, reserving 120ml (½ cup) of the pasta water. If using dried pasta, cook following the timings on the pack.

Pour the artichoke and olive oil mixture into the hot pan with the reserved water and the butter and place over a low heat. Heat gently until the butter has melted, then simmer for 5 minutes.

Add the warm pasta to the pan with the peas and cavolo nero. Shred the basil leaves into the pan, season and grate over the Parmesan. Stir everything together then spoon into warm bowls and serve.

Napa is of course famous for producing beautiful wines but it also happens to have some of the greatest restaurants in the world, and the food markets to go with them. Oxbow Public Market is just one of them: not only is it a great place to sample beer and food, you can buy some pretty good stuff too, including home-cured lamb bacon, which was off the scale! It's made from the belly of lamb rather than the loin, and crisps up really nicely. The fat in the dressing was also delicious.

LAMB BACON, FIG & FETA SALAD

SERVES 6

200g (7 oz) whole lamb bacon rashers or good-quality maple-glazed streaky bacon rashers, halved
1 medium baguette, sliced into 12 rounds on the diagonal
12 ripe figs, 6 halved and 6 whole
4 tablespoons olive oil
4 tablespoons champagne vinegar
4 tablespoons maple syrup
1 small radicchio
4 little gem lettuce
sea salt and freshly ground black pepper
100g (¾ cup) feta cheese

Place a large heavy-based frying pan over a medium heat. When the pan is hot, dry-fry the bacon in batches until crispy. Lift out of the pan and spoon into a bowl.

Fry the slices of baguette in the same pan, again in batches, and add to the bowl with the bacon.

In the same pan, sear the figs, cut-side down if halved, for a few seconds, then add to the bowl.

Reduce the heat slightly and pour the oil, vinegar and maple syrup into the pan with 1 tablespoon water and warm through.

Tear the leaves from the radicchio to separate them and arrange on a large platter. Do the same with the little gem lettuce. Spoon over the figs, baguette 'croutons' and bacon.

Pour the bacon fat from the bowl into the pan with the dressing, season with salt and pepper and stir again, then drizzle over the salad.

Crumble the feta over the top and serve.

This not the first time that I've used Douglas Fir to cook with – it's brilliant to flavour barbecue charcoal and I've also used it in desserts. Ranch dressing is a much more familiar staple in the US and can be made in a variety of different ways. I think it's best to use buttermilk, as it tastes slightly sour.

DOUGLAS FIR PINE POUSSIN SALAD
WITH RANCH DRESSING

=== SERVES 4 ===

For the poussin
1 bunch of Douglas fir pine
3 poussin
4 tablespoons olive oil
sea salt and freshly ground
  black pepper

For the ranch dressing
1 teaspoon garlic purée
1 small white onion,
  finely chopped
small bunch of parsley,
  chives and mint,
  finely chopped
2 teaspoons English
  mustard powder
250ml (1 cup) buttermilk

For the salad
200g (7 oz) Tenderstem
  broccoli
handful of kale leaves
2 tablespoons olive oil
1 garlic cheese bread
handful of dandelion leaves
8 ripe figs, halved
50g (1¾ oz) seedless white
  grapes, halved

Preheat the barbecue: when the coals are silvery in colour, it's ready. Add the Douglas fir pine to the coals, keeping back a small amount to use as a brush.

Prepare the Tenderstem broccoli for the salad. Bring a medium saucepan of water to the boil. Once the water is boiling, blanch the broccoli for 2 minutes then drain and immediately plunge into a bowl of cold water to refresh.

Put the poussin on a board and cut through the back of each bird. Turn over, open each one out then flatten by pressing down on the breast bone. Brush with oil and season. Place on the barbecue (or on a large hot char-grill pan). Cook for 25–30 minutes, turning halfway, until cooked through. Place on a board to rest.

To make the ranch dressing, put all the ingredients into a bowl and season with salt and pepper. Whisk everything together.

Drizzle the Tenderstem broccoli and kale with oil, place onto the barbecue with the bread and cook for 1–2 minutes until charred.

Place the dandelion leaves on a large platter, top with the Tenderstem broccoli and kale. Cut the bread into large chunks and toss in.

Cut each poussin into four pieces, season and pop back on the barbecue for a final 5 minutes to warm through.

Arrange the poussin on top with the figs then scatter over the grapes. Drizzle the ranch dressing over the top and serve.

This dish was famously created at the Waldorf–Astoria hotel in New York in 1896, not by a chef, but by the restaurant manager. It's not classically served with chicken, but I couldn't resist. Cooking the chicken with maple syrup adds a lot of flavour – just be careful it doesn't burn. Ideally, I like to cook it in the oven first then finish it off on the barbecue.

WALDORF SALAD
WITH MAPLE, LEMON & TARRAGON CHICKEN

===== SERVES 4 =====

1.5kg (3 lb) corn-fed chicken, spatchcocked (see tip below)
2 lemons, juiced
small bunch of tarragon
250ml (1 cup) vegetable oil
100ml (½ cup) maple syrup
sea salt and freshly ground black pepper
2 medium egg yolks
1 tablespoon white wine vinegar
1 tablespoon Dijon mustard
4 little gem lettuce, quartered
100g (3½ oz) walnut halves
100g (3½ oz) red grapes
3 celery sticks
1 teaspoon celery salt
2 apples, thinly sliced
a few celery leaves

Preheat the oven to 200°C/400°F/gas mark 6.

Place the chicken in a large roasting tray and pour over the lemon juice. Tear the tarragon into pieces then sprinkle all over the bird. Drizzle 4 tablespoons oil and the maple syrup over the top, then pour 200ml (1 cup) water into the bottom of the tray. Season the chicken well and place in the oven to roast for 45 minutes.

Put the egg yolks into the bowl of a small food blender, then add the vinegar and mustard. Whiz together, and with the motor still running, slowly add the remaining oil until the mixture becomes thick and creamy.

Place the lettuce in a large bowl with the walnuts, grapes and celery. Add the celery salt to the mayo, whiz again to combine, then pour into the bowl, season and mix together.

Pile the salad onto a platter and scatter the apple and celery leaves over the top. Baste the chicken with the juices in the pan and place it whole on top of the salad and serve.

JAMES' TIP
To spatchcock the chicken, put it on a board breast-side down. Take a sharp pair of scissors and cut along the backbone one way then turn the chicken round and cut along the backbone the other way to remove it completely. Turn the chicken over and press down on the breast bone to flatten it out as much as possible.

I was inspired to make this dish while waiting on a beach for Wendy Ida, a famous Californian fitness instructor. In her sixties, Wendy has an infectious personality and her body is testament to her hard work and dedication. What a wonderful person, and the salad's not bad either!

AMERICAN BEER NOODLES
WITH SEARED BEEF & VIETNAMESE BASIL

=== SERVES 4 ===

568ml (19 fl oz) bottle of bitter
400ml (1¾ cups) hot beef stock
100g (3½ oz) udon noodles
4 tablespoons sesame seeds
3 garlic cloves, crushed
4cm (1½ in) piece fresh root
  ginger, peeled and diced
sea salt
2 tablespoons palm sugar
2 red chillies, chopped
large bunch of coriander
  (cilantro), chopped
small bunch of Vietnamese
  basil, chopped
1 tablespoon toasted sesame oil
2 tablespoons soy sauce
3 limes, zested and juiced
2 tablespoons olive oil
knob of butter
4 x 150g (5¼ oz) fillet of beef
  steaks, cut from the centre
  of the fillet

Pour the beer and stock into a pan and bring to the boil. Add the noodles, stir in and cook following the instructions on the pack, around 9 minutes.

In a large non-stick frying pan, toast off the sesame seeds then tip onto paper.

With a large pestle and mortar, pound the garlic and ginger together with a pinch of salt. Add the palm sugar and continue to pound the ingredients together for a minute or two. Add half the chilli, pound again, then finish with half the coriander (cilantro) and half the basil. Pound again for a further minute. Add half the sesame oil, half the soy sauce, lime zest and half the juice and stir.

Drain the noodles and return to the pan then run cold water over them to cool quickly. Drain again, pop back into the pan and tip in the dressing. Give everything a good stir to coat the noodles in the dressing, then add half the remaining coriander and basil.

Place a large non-stick frying pan over a medium heat and drizzle in the oil. When the oil is very hot, add the butter. As soon as the butter has melted, lay the steaks in the pan. Cook for a minute or two on each side until seared. Drizzle over the remaining soy sauce and sesame oil and spoon any juices in the pan to baste. Lift the steaks onto a board, cover and leave to rest. Pour the juices from the pan over the noodles and mix in.

Spoon the noodles onto a large platter. Slice the beef into thick fingers across the grain and place on top. Pour the remaining lime juice over the top. Add the remaining chilli and sprinkle over with the last of the herbs and the sesame seeds.

There are times in life that you look back and say 'Today was a good day' – this was one of them. At Fenway Park, the Boston Red Sox stadium, not only did I hit a home run, but I was also invited to change the scoreboard and write my name on the wall with a marker pen: James Martin woz 'ere.

WARM LOBSTER MACKEREL SALAD
WITH PICKLED TURNIP & RHUBARB

=== SERVES 2 ===

2 tablespoons cider vinegar
2 tablespoons caster (superfine) sugar
1 teaspoon salt
4 red turnips or radishes, sliced very thinly (preferably with a mandolin)
3 x 20cm (8 in) sticks of young rhubarb, cut on the diagonal into 2cm (¾ in) pieces
sea salt and freshly ground black pepper
1 cooked lobster, meat removed from the shell
1 tablespoon micro salad leaves
a few leaves of hyssop (optional)
1 tablespoon olive oil
1 tablespoon butter
150g (5¼ oz) mackerel, filleted and pin-boned
1 small shallot
¼ apple, thinly sliced and chopped into julienne strips

For the mayonnaise
1 large egg yolk
1 teaspoon Dijon mustard
100ml (½ cup) light olive oil
½ lemon, juiced

Put the vinegar, sugar and salt into a pan and place over a medium heat. Once the sugar has dissolved, bring to the boil. Add the turnip (or radish) and rhubarb pieces to the vinegar mixture and take the pan off the heat. Season with salt and pepper.

To make the mayonnaise, put the egg yolk and mustard into a medium bowl and whisk together. Slowly add the oil, starting with a drop at a time, and whisk continuously until the mixture starts to thicken and emulsify. Continue to whisk, pouring the oil in at a steady drizzle now until all the oil has been added. Finish by whisking in the lemon juice, and season.

Spoon the lobster meat into the bowl of mayonnaise. Add the micro salad leaves and hyssop (if using). Fold everything together.

In a non-stick frying pan, heat the oil and butter over a medium heat until the butter is foaming. Lay the mackerel fillets into the pan, skin-side down, and hold flat for 30 seconds. Season and cook for 2–3 minutes then flip over and take the pan off the heat.

Strain the pickled turnip and rhubarb. Line a plate with kitchen paper and spread the vegetables out over it to drain well.

To serve, place a 12cm (4¾ in) ring onto a large plate and lay a quarter of the turnip slices, slightly overlapping, all around it. Remove the ring. Make another circle in the centre, overlapping the other circle, so you've used about half the turnip slices. Do the same again on another plate with the remaining turnip.

Spoon half the lobster salad in the middle of each plate and top each with a mackerel fillet and a few more leaves of hyssop (if using). Slice the shallot into rings and arrange on top with the pickled rhubarb and turnip and the apple.

We definitely need to eat more of these little fellas, as American crayfish have taken over from the UK crayfish in our rivers and streams. It's easy to find containers of the cooked tails in the supermarket. This pasta dish is so simple to make and uses American kale, also called 'black cabbage' or cavolo nero.

BOW PASTA WITH CLAMS, CRAYFISH & CAJUN SPICES

SERVES 6

1 tablespoon salt
500g (1 lb 2 oz) bow pasta
1 teaspoon smoked paprika
1 teaspoon ground white pepper
1 teaspoon dried thyme
1 teaspoon dried oregano
1 teaspoon celery salt
4 tablespoons butter
5 garlic cloves, chopped
4 tablespoons white wine
500g (1 lb 2 oz) clams
300ml (1¼ cups) double
    (heavy) cream
large handful of cavolo
    nero, chopped
500g (1 lb 2 oz) crayfish tails
sea salt and freshly ground
    black pepper
10 drops of Tabasco
25g (1 oz) Parmesan cheese

Bring a large saucepan of water to the boil, add the salt and the pasta, stir in and simmer for 10 minutes until al dente.

Mix the paprika, white pepper, thyme, oregano and celery salt together in a bowl.

Melt the butter in a large pan over a low to medium heat. Once the butter has stopped foaming, add the garlic, herbs and spices and cook for a minute or two. Pour in the white wine, then add the clams and cream and bring to the boil. Cover with a lid and cook for 2 minutes.

As the clams start to open, add the cavolo nero followed by the crayfish. Bring to the boil and simmer for 2 minutes.

Drain the pasta, keeping a little of the water, and tip into the pan with the sauce. Season and keep cooking for another 2 minutes. Add the Tabasco and grate half the Parmesan into the sauce. Spoon onto a large serving bowl and grate over the rest of the cheese.

This pasta sauce uses the ingredients from a Bloody Mary cocktail. I cooked it in the middle of the chilli plantation famous for making the Tabasco sauce that every cook has in their larder. The chilli peppers are hand-picked and then mixed with salt to create a 'mash'. The mash is placed in old bourbon barrels, covered and left for three years to mature. Just before bottling, it's mixed with vinegar. That's all there is to it – just three ingredients.

PASTA WITH BLOODY MARY SAUCE

⟹ SERVES 6 ⟸

1 tablespoon sea salt
300g (10½ oz) dried farfalle pasta
4 tablespoons olive oil
100g (3½ oz) fresh breadcrumbs
small bunch of flat-leaf parsley, finely chopped
600g (1 lb 5 oz) raw prawns (shrimp), peeled, de-veined and butterflied

For the Bloody Mary sauce
1 red onion, diced
1 teaspoon caster (superfine) sugar
1 teaspoon celery salt
sea salt and freshly ground black pepper
3 garlic cloves, chopped
4 tablespoons Worcestershire sauce
15 drops of Tabasco
4 tablespoons vodka
2 x 400g (14 oz) tins chopped tomatoes

Bring a large saucepan of water to the boil then add the salt and pasta. Stir the pasta through the water to loosen the pieces then cook according to the timings on the pack.

Meanwhile, heat a frying pan until hot, add half the oil then stir in the breadcrumbs. Cook until the breadcrumbs are golden and crispy, then add the parsley to the pan. You should hear it pop when it crisps up. Spoon the mixture into a bowl and set aside.

To make the sauce, drizzle the remaining oil into the same frying pan. Stir in the onion and cook, stirring occasionally, for around 5 minutes. Sprinkle over the sugar, celery salt and season well then add the garlic. Stir everything together and cook over a medium heat for 1 minute. Stir in the Worcestershire sauce and Tabasco.

Pour the vodka into the sauce and light with a match (flambé) to burn off the alcohol. Add the tomatoes, then wash out the juices in the tin with 100ml (½ cup) water. Pour this into the sauce and stir in then finally stir in the prawns (shrimp). Simmer over a low to medium heat for 5 minutes.

Strain 100ml (½ cup) of the cooking water into a jug or bowl and reserve, then drain the rest of the pasta. Stir the pasta through the tomato sauce with the reserved cooking water. Taste to check the seasoning.

Spoon the pasta onto a large platter, sprinkle over the parsley breadcrumbs and serve straight away.

Salem is of course famous for witches and witchcraft, but it's also famous for pumpkins – they were everywhere! We cooked near the Witch House, the former home of a judge involved in the 1692 witch trials. We also have Salem to thank for some ingenious inventors. Moses Farmer was the first to light his house (on Salem's Pearl Street) with electricity, and later sold his lightbulb design to Thomas Edison. Alexander Graham Bell invented the telephone in Salem, and it was here that the first call was made.

SPICED CHICKEN
WITH MUSHROOMS, PUMPKIN & PASTA

SERVES 4–6

1 teaspoon dried ginger pieces or ½ teaspoon ground ginger
2 tablespoons olive oil
100g (3½ oz) bacon lardons
1 chicken (around 1.3kg/3 lb), jointed into 8 pieces
100g (3½ oz) baby onions
sea salt and freshly ground black pepper
4 garlic cloves, crushed
200g (7 oz) pumpkin or butternut squash, chopped into 2cm (¾ in) cubes
300ml (1¼ cups) hot chicken stock
4 tablespoons white wine
100ml (½ cup) double (heavy) cream
3 star anise
200g (7 oz) chicken of the woods mushrooms, shredded
1 teaspoon sea salt
200g (7 oz) fresh green fusilli pasta
100g (¾ cup) butter, chopped
small bunch of parsley, chopped
small bunch of tarragon, leaves picked and chopped
1 teaspoon nigella seeds

Put the dried ginger into a small bowl, cover with cold water and leave to soak for 10 minutes to rehydrate it.

Heat the oil in a large casserole dish then add the lardons and cook for 2–3 minutes over a medium heat until crispy. Add the chicken pieces and the baby onions, season well and cook for a further 5 minutes, turning the chicken over as necessary until golden.

Add the ginger, garlic, pumpkin, stock, wine, cream and star anise and bring to the boil. Stir in the mushrooms and cook for a further 10 minutes.

Meanwhile, bring a large saucepan of water to the boil then add the salt and the pasta. Stir the pasta through the water to loosen the pieces, then cook for 2 minutes. Strain 100ml (½ cup) of the cooking water into a jug or bowl and set aside, then drain the rest of the pasta.

Stir the pasta into the pan with the chicken, along with the butter and reserved cooking water to loosen the sauce. Lift out and discard the star anise then season and sprinkle over the herbs and nigella seeds. Spoon the chicken, pasta and sauce onto a large sharing platter and serve.

DESSERTS

I can't really blame these doughnuts for my lack of surfing prowess, but I do blame dishes like this for not being able to get into a size XL wet suit! Skyler the surfing dog is a local Santa Cruz legend who put me to shame on a surfboard. Surfing was fun, but I think I'll stick to eating doughnuts.

DOUGHNUTS
WITH STRAWBERRIES & ICE CREAM

=== MAKES 12 ===

For the doughnuts
500g (3½ cups) strong
   white bread flour,
   plus extra for dusting
1 teaspoon salt
1 tablespoon caster
   (superfine) sugar,
   plus extra for sprinkling
4 tablespoons butter,
   at room temperature
300ml (1¼ cups) milk
1 medium egg, beaten
7g (¼ oz) fresh yeast
   (or 1 teaspoon dried yeast)
1 litre (5 cups) vegetable oil,
   for deep-frying

For the compote
300g (10½ oz) strawberries,
   hulled and quartered
2 tablespoons caster
   (superfine) sugar
4 tablespoons water
   or the juice of 1 lemon

To serve
vanilla ice cream

Place the flour, salt and sugar in the bowl of a freestanding mixer fitted with a dough hook.

Put the butter and milk into a medium saucepan and place over a low heat. Heat until the milk reaches body temperature then crumble the yeast into the pan and stir into the milk and butter.

Pour the yeast mixture into the dry ingredients with the egg. Mix at a medium speed for 2–3 minutes until a dough forms. Alternatively, knead by hand for 15 minutes. Cover with clingfilm (plastic wrap) and leave to rise for 1 hour.

To make the compote, put the strawberries in a saucepan with the sugar and the water or lemon juice. Bring to the boil and simmer for 3–4 minutes.

Dust a board with flour and tip the dough out onto it. Knead lightly to bring the dough together then cut the dough into 12 pieces and shape – into small balls, for instance, or rings.

Heat the vegetable oil in a deep-fat fryer to 150°C/300°F or in a deep heavy-based saucepan until a breadcrumb sizzles and turns brown when dropped into it. Note: hot oil can be dangerous; do not leave it unattended.

Cook the balls of dough in batches, three or four at a time. The dough will double once they start to cook. Fry gently so that they cook all the way through, around 3 minutes for the rings and 4–5 minutes for the balls, flipping halfway through.

Drain on a plate lined with kitchen paper and dust with caster (superfine) sugar. Once all of them have been cooked, transfer to a plate, spoon the compote over them and serve with ice cream.

This is an all-American classic chocolate dessert. Simple to prepare, so most households will have this on their menu.

CHOCOLATE CREAM PIE

≡ SERVES 8 ≡

For the crust
100g (3½ oz) water biscuits
50g (3½ tablespoons) butter

For the filling
500ml (18 fl oz) milk
1 tablespoon butter
150g (¾ cup) caster
   (superfine) sugar
2 teaspoons vanilla extract
6 medium egg yolks
6 tablespoons cornflour
   (cornstarch)
2 teaspoons cocoa powder
½ teaspoon salt
750ml (3 cups) double
   (heavy) cream
4 tablespoons bourbon whiskey
25g (1 oz) dark chocolate,
   70% cocoa solids, grated

Line a loose-bottomed fluted tart tin, 22cm (8½ in) across and 4cm (1½ in) deep, with baking parchment.

Make the crust. Put the water biscuits into the bowl of a food processor and blitz until very fine. Melt the butter in a medium pan over a low heat, then stir in the blitzed biscuits. Spoon into the tin and press down into the base. Cover with clingfilm (plastic wrap) and press down firmly with your hands.

Pour the milk into a large saucepan and add the butter, sugar and 1 teaspoon of the vanilla extract. Heat over a low heat until the butter has melted and the sugar has dissolved.

In a large bowl, whisk together the egg yolks, cornflour (cornstarch), cocoa powder and half the milk to make a paste. Pour this mixture back into a clean pan and pour in the remaining milk mixture. Whisk continuously for around 2–3 minutes until the mixture thickens.

Pour the filling into the tart tin so that it covers the biscuit base. Transfer to the fridge and chill for 1–2 hours.

Pour the cream into a bowl with the remaining teaspoon of vanilla extract and the bourbon and whisk until soft peaks form. Spoon the cream into a piping bag fitted with a 1cm (½ in) circular plain or fluted nozzle. Pipe the cream into rosettes all over the chocolate filling then scatter the grated chocolate over the top.

Take the tart out of the tin and place on a large plate. For a really clean cut, heat the knife so it cuts through the cream and custard easily. To do this, pour boiling water over a large chopping knife and wipe dry. Use the knife while it is still hot, and cut as many slices as you need to.

Based on a hot chocolate fondant, these are cooked with a hint of chilli, which adds a nice kick.

MOLTEN CHOCOLATE S'MORES

For the cake
125g (½ cup plus 1 tablespoon) butter, chopped, plus extra for greasing
125g (4½ oz) dark chocolate, 70% cocoa solids, broken into pieces
4 medium eggs
100g (½ cup) caster (superfine) sugar
100g (¾ cup) plain (all-purpose) flour
1 red chilli, chopped

For the chocolate sauce
50g (¼ cup) caster (superfine) sugar
100g (3½ oz) dark chocolate, 70% cocoa solids, broken into pieces
knob of butter

For the caramel sauce
150g (¾ cup) caster (superfine) sugar
2 tablespoons butter
100ml (½ cup) double (heavy) cream

To serve
200ml (1 cup) double (heavy) cream
3 digestive biscuits (graham crackers), crushed
6 large marshmallows
1 tablespoon cocoa powder

Preheat the oven to 180°C/350°F/gas mark 4. Grease six 7.5cm (3 in) mini pudding moulds.

Melt the butter and chocolate in a bain-marie (a large bowl resting over a pan of just-simmering water), making sure the base doesn't touch the water. Cool a little.

In a separate large bowl, whisk the eggs and sugar together for 1 minute. Then carefully pour in the chocolate and butter mix. Whisk together, then fold in the flour with a large metal spoon. Pour the mixture evenly among the greased moulds, then sprinkle in the chilli. Bake for 9 minutes.

To make the chocolate sauce, put 4 tablespoons of water into a medium pan with the caster (superfine) sugar and the chocolate. Place the pan over a medium heat and bring to the boil, whisking continuously. Add the knob of butter and whisk in.

For the caramel sauce, put the sugar into a medium heavy-based pan and place over a low to medium heat, without stirring, until the sugar dissolves and turns golden brown. Add the butter and cream to the pan – stand back at this point as the hot sugar will splutter. Turn down the heat a little and whisk everything together until smooth. Take the pan off the heat.

To serve, drizzle the caramel sauce and the chocolate sauce over a large platter then let them cool slightly. Drizzle over the remaining 200ml (1 cup) double (heavy) cream. Loosen by running a knife around the edge, then take the fondants out of the pudding moulds and place on the platter. Sprinkle the crushed biscuits over the top and pile the whipped cream around them. Scorch the marshmallows on a baking sheet using a blowtorch and place on the platter between the fondants. Finally, dust everything with cocoa powder.

This cake was inspired by our trip to San Antonio, and something I tasted at a churros stand, as a mariachi band was firing up. Mexican in origin, and rich in cinnamon, the sauce has to be made with goat's milk and no other. La Margarita is a must for Mexican food. The restaurant, which must seat 600, is open 24 hours a day, 7 days a week – nuts!

APPLE CAKE
WITH CAJETA SAUCE

SERVES 6

For the cake
200g (¾ cup plus 2 tablespoons) butter, softened, plus extra for greasing
200g (1 cup) caster (superfine) sugar
1 teaspoon vanilla extract
4 medium eggs
200g (1½ cups) self-raising (self-rising) flour
2 Cox's apples

For the cajeta sauce
500ml (18 fl oz) goat's milk
200g (1 cup) caster (superfine) sugar
3 cinnamon sticks, broken in half
1 teaspoon vanilla extract
1 teaspoon bicarbonate of soda (baking soda)
50g (1¾ oz) pecans

To serve
vanilla ice cream

Preheat the oven to 180°C/350°F/gas mark 4. Grease a 22cm (8½ in) savarin tin with a little butter.

First make the cajeta sauce. Pour the milk into a deep saucepan, add the sugar and cinnamon and bring to the boil. Add the vanilla extract, then whisk in the bicarbonate of soda (baking soda) – the mixture will froth up but just keep stirring it in. Turn down the heat a little and simmer for 20 minutes, stirring occasionally.

Make the cake. Put the butter, sugar and vanilla extract into the bowl of a freestanding mixer and beat with a K beater until the mixture turns from creamy to white. Add the eggs to the bowl, one at a time, while mixing, then add the flour and mix gently together. Turn up the speed and whisk fast for 1 minute until the mixture is completely combined.

Core one of the apples, slice very thinly and overlap the slices over the bottom of the tin until it is covered. Spoon the cake mixture evenly on top and smooth down with a metal spoon. Drop on a board to knock the batter down, then place on a baking sheet and bake for 45 minutes to 1 hour. To check the cake is cooked, insert a skewer and pull it out. It's ready when it comes out clean. Take out of the oven and cool on a wire rack.

Once the cake has cooled, upturn it on a cake stand or serving plate and fill the centre with ice cream.

Core then cut the remaining apple into thin slices. While the sauce is still warm, sieve it into a clean pan. Add the apple and pecans and stir in, then spoon over the cake and serve.

This dish was created at Brennan's in New Orleans in the 1950s, for the crime commissioner at the time. We saw it being served at the Palace Café, a fantastic old-school place with chefs' hats, penguin waiters and top-class service, with food from another era. The chef cooked me blackened fish with spices, and while I waited for it, I watched the front-of-house team serving this classic banana dish. There, they make it on gueridon trolleys, pushing them around the restaurant, but doing it in the comfort of your own home is much easier! This must be served hot. I've put *pain perdu* with it but pancakes would also be delicious. It wouldn't traditionally be served with whipped cream and pecans, but it works.

BANANAS FOSTER

SERVES 3

3 medium eggs
2 tablespoons caster (superfine) sugar
4 tablespoons milk
4 tablespoons butter
3 thick slices of brioche, cut from a loaf
5 bananas, peeled
4 tablespoons dark brown sugar
¼ teaspoon ground cinnamon
2 tablespoons banana liqueur
2 tablespoons rum
25g (1 oz) pecans
300ml (1¼ cups) carton double (heavy) cream, whipped and chilled
3 scoops vanilla ice cream

Put the eggs, caster (superfine) sugar and the milk into a bowl and whisk together.

Place a large frying pan over a low to medium heat and add 2 tablespoons butter. Dip the brioche into the egg mixture, and once the butter has melted, place the brioche into the hot pan. Cook for 1 minute on each side until golden brown. Transfer the pieces to a warm plate.

Wipe the pan clean, then return it to the heat and add the remaining butter. Once the butter has melted, add the bananas, keeping them whole. Cook until golden brown on one side, sprinkle with half the brown sugar, then flip the bananas over. Sprinkle the remaining sugar over the top, add the cinnamon then pour in the banana liqueur and rum. Flame to burn off the alcohol. Simmer for a couple of minutes until the butter and sugar turns into a sauce, then stir in the pecans.

Spoon the bananas and the sauce all over the brioche, then top with the whipped cream and the ice cream.

Another classic American dessert, this moreish tart is packed with crunchy pecans, smothered in bourbon-flavoured sticky goodness. If you'd like to glaze the cake, warm 2 tablespoons golden syrup (light corn syrup) in a pan and brush all over the tart after baking.

BOURBON PECAN TART

=== SERVES 8 ===

For the pastry
250g (1¾ cups plus 2 tablespoons) plain (all-purpose) flour, plus extra for rolling out
125g (½ cup plus 1 tablespoon) butter, diced, at room temperature
1 medium egg, beaten

For the filling
4 tablespoons butter
100g (3½ oz) treacle
4 medium eggs
175g (¾ cup plus 2 tablespoons) caster (superfine) sugar
1 teaspoon ground cinnamon
6 tablespoons bourbon whiskey
500g (1 lb 2 oz) pecans

To serve
double (heavy) cream or vanilla ice cream

To make the pastry, put the flour into a large bowl, add the butter and rub in using your fingertips until the mixture resembles breadcrumbs. Pour the egg into the middle of the mixture and stir in well, then lightly knead the mixture to bring it together. Add 1 tablespoon of water if the mixture feels a bit dry and doesn't come together into a smooth dough. Shape the dough into a disc, wrap in clingfilm (plastic wrap) and rest in the fridge for 20 minutes.

Lightly flour a clean work surface then roll out the pastry into a large circle, around 2mm (⅛ in) thick. Keep turning the pastry every time you roll it to keep the shape even. Use to line a 26cm (10 in) fluted loose-bottomed tart tin, 3cm (1¼ in) deep.

Line the tin with the pastry. Press into the flutes and edge of the base of the tin, then leave the remainder hanging over the edge.

Preheat the oven to 160°C/325°F/gas mark 3.

Make the filling. Put the butter and treacle into a small pan and heat gently to melt the butter. Stir together. Take the pan off the heat and cool a little.

Whisk the eggs and sugar together in a large bowl until mixed well then pour in the cooled butter mixture, cinnamon and bourbon and stir everything together.

Put the tart tin on a baking sheet. Spread the pecans all over the tart case, then pour the filling over the top. Bake for 35–45 minutes until the filling is firm.

Once cooked, cut all the overhanging edges off the tart using a sharp serrated knife. Cool the tart until warm, then lift the tart out of the tin and transfer to a plate.

Cut the tart into slices and serve with cream or ice cream.

Borden's ice cream parlour in Lafayette is a must for anyone who loves their ice cream. After enjoying a main course at nearby Johnson's Boucanière, walk over to Borden's and try one of the large cones.

ICE CREAM BROWNIE CAKE

=== SERVES 6 ===

For the brownies
185g (¾ cup plus 2 teaspoons) butter, cubed, plus extra for greasing
185g (6½ oz) dark chocolate, 70% cocoa solids, chopped
3 eggs
270g (1½ cups minus 2 tablespoons) caster (superfine) sugar
85g (⅔ cup) plain (all-purpose) flour
40g (½ cups) cocoa powder

For the ice creams
150g (5¼ oz) vanilla
150g (5¼ oz) mint choc chip
150g (5¼ oz) strawberry

For the Italian meringue
200g (1 cup) caster (superfine) sugar
4 medium egg whites

Preheat the oven to 160°C/325°F/gas mark 3. Grease and line a 30 x 20cm (12 x 8 in) lipped baking tray with baking parchment.

Melt the chocolate and butter in a bain-marie (a large bowl resting over a pan of just-simmering water), making sure the base doesn't touch the water. Set aside to cool to room temperature.

Put the eggs into a separate bowl and add 90g (7 tablespoons) of the sugar. Whisk using an electric hand whisk (or a freestanding mixer fitted with the balloon whisk) until it is light and fluffy and leaves a ribbon-like trail when the beaters are lifted. Pour the chocolate and butter mixture into the eggs, add the remaining sugar, then sift in the flour and cocoa. Use a large metal spoon to fold together thoroughly. Pour half the mixture into the lined tray, spread evenly and bake for 13–15 minutes. Lift the brownie, with the lining paper, onto a wire rack. Re-line the tray and spoon the rest of the mixture in, working quickly. Bake as before.

Using a 15cm (6 in) plate, cut four rounds out of the brownie. Place one round onto a large flat plate. Working quickly, spread the vanilla ice cream on top, not quite up to the edge. Place another round on top and layer up the different flavoured ice creams, ending with a brownie round on top. Freeze for 1 hour.

Half an hour into the freezing, make the meringue. Put the sugar into a saucepan and pour in 100ml (½ cup) water. Heat gently to dissolve the sugar then bring to the boil and cook until the syrup reaches 120°C/250°F (or soft ball stage). Whisk the egg whites in a spotlessly clean bowl (or use a freestanding mixer) until very firm. Continue to whisk while pouring the boiling sugar into the side of the bowl, keeping clear of the beaters. Continue to whisk until the meringue is cool, thick and glossy. Spoon into a large piping bag fitted with a 1cm (½ in) plain nozzle. Pipe all over the cake then blowtorch until golden brown. Serve straight away.

Strictly for grown-ups... I don't advise eating these delicious fluffins too close to bedtime: the dulce de leche and marshmallow fluff combine to give quite a sugar hit!

BOSTON FLUFFINS

For the muffins
2 medium eggs
125ml (½ cup) vegetable oil
250ml (1 cup) milk
200g (1 cup) caster
   (superfine) sugar
400g (3 cups) self-raising
   (self-rising) flour
1 teaspoon salt
1 tablespoon gin
2 tablespoons pecans, chopped
2 extra-large marshmallows

To decorate
100g (3½ oz) dulce de leche
   caramel sauce
4 tablespoons pecans, chopped
100g (3½ oz) marshmallow fluff

Preheat the oven to 180°C/350°F/gas mark 4. Grease the holes of a 12-hole silicone muffin tin or line a metal one with paper cases.

Put the eggs into a large bowl. Add the oil, milk, sugar, flour and salt and whisk everything together until smooth. Add the gin and the pecans and fold in. Spoon the mixture evenly between the holes in the muffin tin.

Slice the marshmallows into 6 slices each and push one slice into the centre of each portion of batter in the muffin tin. Bake for around 25 minutes.

When the muffins come out of the oven, cool a little, then remove from the tin. Place each on a plate, spoon over the caramel sauce and sprinkle over the nuts. To finish, top with a dollop of fluff, and brown the tops with a blowtorch if you have one to hand.

Using purple food colouring in this angel cake gives a blueberry effect,
but allows the texture of the cake to remain light and fluffy.

MARBLED ANGEL CAKE
WITH PEACH, FIG & CHAMPAGNE

SERVES 6–8

For the cake
255g (1 cup plus 2 tablespoons)
  butter, softened, plus extra
  for greasing
255g (1¼ cups) caster
  (superfine) sugar
1 teaspoon vanilla extract
5 medium eggs
225g (1¾ cups) self-raising
  (self-rising) flour, sifted
a few drops of purple food
  colouring (or the colour
  of your choice)

For the poached fruit
4 peaches, each sliced
  into 8 wedges
6 figs, halved
200ml (1 cup) champagne

To serve
icing (powdered) sugar,
  for dusting
300ml (1¼ cups) whipped
  double (heavy) cream

Preheat the oven to 180°C/350°F/gas mark 4. Grease a 22cm
(8½ in) bundt tin.

Put the butter into a large bowl and add the sugar and vanilla
extract. Beat together until the mixture is pale, light and fluffy.
This will take 3–4 minutes.

Add the eggs, one at a time, to the creamed butter mixture,
mixing well between each addition. Tip the flour into the bowl
and mix on a slow speed for 30 seconds then increase the speed
and beat on high for 10 seconds. Put a quarter of the mixture into
a small bowl and add the food colouring. Mix thoroughly. Spoon
the coloured mixture back into the bowl with the plain cake mixture
and stir twice to marble the colour through the plain part.

Spoon the cake mixture into the tin, smooth the surface,
then bake for 40 minutes. Allow to cool for 10 minutes in the
tin then turn out onto a wire rack to cool completely.

While the cake is baking, poach the fruit. Place the peaches
and figs into a medium pan, pour the champagne over the top and
bring to a gentle simmer. Simmer for 5 minutes then set aside.

To serve, put the cake on a large plate, dust with icing
(powdered) sugar and serve with a bowl of the fruit and the
whipped cream.

These are a *must* if you travel to Philadelphia, and are the city's sweet street food of choice. A cross between a doughnut and churros, these are usually made in a funnel (yes, that's a funnel). As most of my funnels are kept in the garage and smell of Castrol GTX rather than olive oil, I thought it best to use a piping bag. These cakes are normally just served sprinkled with icing (powdered) sugar and eaten on the move.

FUNNEL CAKES
WITH BLUEBERRY & GIN COMPOTE

SERVES 6

For the cakes
1 litre (5 cups) vegetable oil, for frying
1 teaspoon salt
2 teaspoons baking powder
450g (3½ cups) plain (all-purpose) flour
3 medium eggs
4 tablespoons caster (superfine) sugar
450ml (2 cups) milk
2 tablespoons gin
icing (powdered) sugar, for dusting

For the compote
300g (2¼ cups) blueberries
4 tablespoons gin

Make the compote. Put the blueberries and gin into a pan and heat gently for around 5–6 minutes until the blueberries have cooked down.

Heat the vegetable oil in a deep-fat fryer to 175°C/350°F or in a deep heavy-based saucepan until a breadcrumb sizzles and turns brown when dropped into it. Note: hot oil can be dangerous; do not leave it unattended.

Put the salt into a large bowl. Add the baking powder, flour, eggs, sugar and milk and whisk until smooth. Pour in the gin and whisk again.

Fit a piping bag with a small plain nozzle (around 7mm/¼ in) and spoon enough mixture to half-fill the bag. Pipe into the hot oil into a round circle shape. When the cake has turned golden brown, turn it over and cook until it turns golden on the other side. It will need about 2 minutes on each side.

Line a large plate with kitchen paper and lift the cake onto it to drain. Fill the bag again and repeat until all the batter is used up and you've made six cakes. Dust the icing (powdered) sugar over the cakes.

Divide the compote among six plates, then top each with a funnel cake and serve.

INDEX

WITH THANKS

To all the chefs, foodies, fixers, suppliers and producers – oh, and a surfing dog – that we met along the road trip, thank you so much for all your help making this show what it is. To the crew from Blue Marlin Television for making this all make sense – half of them have been locked in a dark room editing the footage to make it look like I know what I'm doing. To Kevin Lygo, Helen Warner, Clare Ely, Jane Beacon, and the rest of the team at ITV for letting me go on my travels again after my French adventure. To Amy Christian and all the team at Quadrille for making sense of a dyslexic chef typing madly on a computer. To Smith & Gilmour for such a beautiful book. To Fiona and her team at Limelight who keep me on the road alongside my amazing PA Pippa. To Sam and Chris for putting my madness on the plate again when we got home for this book and for lugging wooden tables and trestles to endless ends of fields on the trip to find the perfect shot to film. To Peter Cassidy, the best snapper in the business: it was great to have you on the tour. But most of all, thank you America, I bloody love ya and I'm definitely coming back!

INDEX & ACKNOWLEDGEMENTS

★ ★